Arthur Henry Messiter

Choir Office-Book

Arthur Henry Messiter

Choir Office-Book

ISBN/EAN: 9783337296742

Printed in Europe, USA, Canada, Australia, Japan

Cover: Foto ©Thomas Meinert / pixelio.de

More available books at **www.hansebooks.com**

Choir Office-Book.

THE

DAILY AND OCCASIONAL OFFICES

AND THE

ORDER OF HOLY COMMUNION

SET TO

ANGLICAN AND PLAIN-SONG MUSIC

AS USED IN

Trinity Church, New York.

EDITED BY

A. H. MESSITER, Mus. Doc.
ORGANIST OF TRINITY CHURCH.

NEW YORK:
E. & J. B. YOUNG & COMPANY,
COOPER UNION, FOURTH AVENUE.
1891.

The Publishers are permitted to print the following Note from the Rector of Trinity Parish.

THIS Choir Office-Book needs no commendation from me, or any one else, to help it on its way through the parishes of the land. Compiled by Dr. Messiter, who completes, this year, a quarter of a century's service as organist of Trinity Church, and published by the Messrs. Young, to whom we owe so much in the line of Church literature, it carries its credentials on its title page, and deserves the welcome prepared for it in advance in our choir-rooms and churches, and in those homes where sacred music is a favorite study, and a delightful recreation.

M. D.

TRINITY RECTORY, February 16, 1891.

PREFACE.

THE Plainsong is the foundation, or first principle, of all music used in the service of the Church. The simplest form of Plainsong consists of a recitation on one note, with an inflection of varying length at the close of each sentence, or at the close of the entire recitation. Certain phrases of this nature have been, from time immemorial, associated with particular parts of the Church service: and, somewhat varied or corrupted in the course of many centuries, still survive: testifying, in their way, to the primitive and Catholic character of the Church which so retains them.

Plainsong includes the Gregorian Tones and the traditional ritual music for the various parts of the Church service: also, Masses and other unharmonized music written in obsolete scales and notation. The Gregorian Tones take their name from Pope Gregory the Great, who reformed and set in order the Church chants of his day, A. D. 590. The Tones, or tunes, themselves are of still greater antiquity; it is claimed that they were used at the consecration of Solomon's Temple: considered musically, they are so rudimentary, that something very similar may easily be supposed to have been used. Originally sung, of necessity, in unison; something of their primitive ruggedness is retained by continuing the unison treatment: but as a more or less free organ accompaniment is usually employed, there seems no reason why vocal harmony should not be also allowed. Practically, it will be found an agreeable relief, and a convenient means of special effect, to sing occasional verses in parts.

By Anglican music, we understand music written for the Eng'ish Church, and to English words: such music being generally in harmony for four or more voices, and consequently in modern scales. These conditions are first found in operation at the English Reformation, when the Church service was translated into the "vulgar tongue," and the Plainsong adapted to English words. Immediately after the publication, in 1550, of the first Prayer-book of Edward the Sixth, with the Plainsong adapted by John Merbecke, leading English musicians set themselves to furnish harmonized settings. Numerous Litanies and sets of Responses were written, mostly founded on the Plainsong, which was assigned to the Tenor voice: as in the service by Tallys, which has come to be accepted as the standard setting. Tallys's responses were, however, not intended for ordinary use: they are called "Extraordinary Responsalls upon Festivalls." The harmonized Ferial Responses and Litany, as given in this book and everywhere sung, have the Plainsong in the Treble, with simple harmonies: Tallys's Litany retains the Plainsong in the Treble, but has elaborate harmonies, which are not only difficult to sing, but require a very deliberate delivery.

A similar process was applied to the Gregorian Tones, which were harmonized with the Plainsong in the Tenor: the Plainsong element was, however, soon dropped, and the present form of the single chant permanently adopted, the Tenor part having no special importance: the double chant was a later development, dating from about 1700. The settings of the Canticles to varied music, technically called "Services," date also from about 1550, Tallys's Service in D-Minor being probably the earliest.

In this book will be found all the Ritual music required for the most elaborate Service of either Anglican or Gregorian systems: with the addition of a few Canticles in Anthem form, selected with a view to general utility: the needs of small Mission Churches have also been considered. The Plainsong is, in all cases, provided with a suggestive accompaniment for the Organ; in some instances for the first time, as in the Offices of Holy Communion and Burial: the Priest's part being in the Tenor, its natural position; and the portions for Choir in the upper part of the accompaniment.

TABLE OF CONTENTS.

		PAGE
THE CANTICLES.	*With Anglican Chants*	2–23
THE PROPER ANTHEMS.	*With Anglican Chants*	24–30
THE CHORAL SERVICE	*Ferial and Festal*	31–39
THE LITANY.	*Ferial and Festal*	39–46
THE HOLY COMMUNION	*Anglican*	46–104
THE HOLY COMMUNION	*Plainsong*	105–129
THE CANTICLES.	*As Anthems*	129–157
THE BURIAL OFFICE	*Anglican*	158–162
THE BURIAL OFFICE.	*Plainsong*	163–167
THE CANTICLES	*Set to Gregorian Tones*	168–207
THE PROPER ANTHEMS	*Set to Gregorian Tones*	208–213
MISERERE	*Plainsong*	214–220
DE PROFUNDIS.	*Plainsong*	221
INDEX		223

Venite.

MORNING PRAYER.

Venite, exultemus Domino.

O COME let us *sing* | un - to the | Lord : let us heartly *rejoice* in the | strength · of | our · sal- | vation.

2 Let us come before His *presence* with | thanks · = | giving : and show *ourselves* | glad · in | Him · with | psalms.

3 For the *Lord* is a | great · = | God : and a *great* | King · a- | bove · all | gods.

4 In His hand are all the *corners* | of · the | earth : and the *strength* of the | hills · is | His · = | also.

5 The sea is *His*, | and · He | made it : and His *hands* pre- | pared · the | dry · = | land.

6 O come let us *worship* | and · fall | down : and *kneel* be- | fore · the | Lord · our | Maker.

7 For He *is* the | Lord . our | God : and we are the people of His pasture, *and* the | sheep · of | His · = | hand.

8 O worship the *Lord* in the | beauty · of | holiness : let the whole *earth* | stand · in | awe · of | Him.

9 For He *cometh*, for He *cometh* to | judge · the | earth: and with righteousness to judge the *world*, and the | peo - ple | with · His | truth.

GLORY be to the *Father*, | and · to the | Son : *and* | to · the | Ho - ly | Ghost ;

As it was in the beginning, is *now*, and | ev - er | shall be : *world* with- | out · end | A · = | men.

Te Deum Laudamus.

BENNETT.

W E *praise* | Thee · O | God : we *acknowledge* | Thee · to | be · the | LORD.
2 All the *earth* doth | wor - ship | Thee : the *Father* | ev - er- | last · = | ing.
3 To Thee all *Angels* | cry · a- | loud : the *Heavens,* and | all · the | powers · there- | in.
4 To Thee *Cherubim* and | Se - raph- | im : *con-* | tin - ual- | ly · do | cry,
5 Holy, | Ho - ly, | Holy : *Lord* | God · of | Sa - ba- | oth ;
6 Heaven and earth are *full* of the | Ma - jes- | ty : *of* | Thy · = | glo · = | ry.
7 The glorious *company* | of · the A- | postles : *praise* | = · = | = · = | Thee.
8 The goodly *fellowship* | of · the | Prophets : *praise* | = · = | = · = | Thee.
9 The noble *army* | of · = | Martyrs : *praise* | = · = | = · = | Thee.
10 The holy Church *throughout* | all · the | world : *doth* | = · ac- | know - ledge | Thee ;
11 The *Father* of an | infi - nite | Majesty ; Thine *adorable* | true · and | on - ly | Son ;
12 *Also* the | Ho - ly | Ghost : *the* | Com · = | = · fort- | er.
13 Thou *art* the | King · of | glory : *O* | = · = | = · = | Christ.
14 Thou art the *ever-* | last - ing | Son : *of* | = · the | Fa · = | ther.

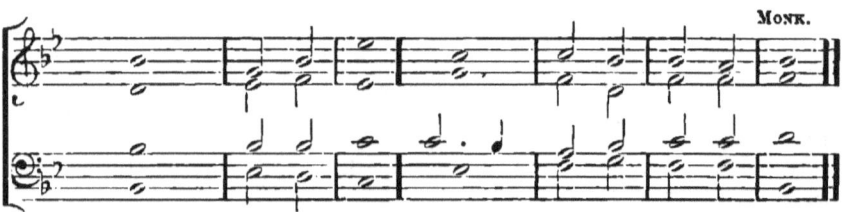

MONK.

15 When Thou tookest upon *Thee* to de- | liv - er | man : Thou didst humble *Thyself* to be | born · = | of · a | Virgin.
16 When Thou hadst *overcome* the | sharp - ness of | death : Thou didst open the Kingdom of *Heaven* to | all · be- | liev · = | ers.
17 Thou sittest at the *right* | hand · of | God : *in* the | glo - ry | of · the | Father.
18 We *believe* that | Thou · shalt | come : *to* | be · = | our · = | judge.
19 We therefore pray *Thee* | help · Thy | servants : whom Thou hast *redeemed* | with, Thy | pre - cious | blood.

20 Make them to be *numbered* | with · Thy | saints : in *glory* | ev - er- | last · = | ing.
21 O *Lord*, | save · Thy | people : *and* | bless · Thine | her - it- | age.
22 Gov- | = · ern | them : *and* | lift · them | up · for | ever.

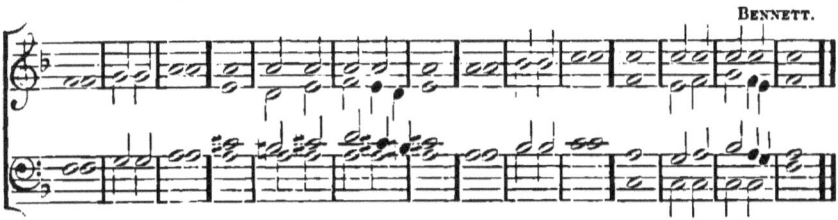

23 *Day* | by · = | day : *we* | mag - ni- | fy · = | Thee.
24 *And* we | worship · Thy | Name : *ever* | world · with- | out · = | end.
25 *Vouch-* | safe · O | LORD : to keep *us* | this · day | with - out | sin.
26 O *Lord*, have | mer - cy up- | on us : *have* | mer - cy up- | on · = | us.
27 O LORD let Thy *mercy* | be · up- | on us : *as* | our · trust | is · in | Thee.
28 O *Lord*, in | Thee have · I | trusted : *let* me | ne - ver | be · con- | founded.

Benedicite, omnia opera Domini.

CAMIDGE.

O ALL ye *Works* of the *Lord,* | bless · ye the | Lord : praise *Him,* and | magni - fy | Him · for | ever.

2 O ye *Angels* of the *Lord,* | bless · ye the | Lord : praise *Him,* and | magni - fy | Him · for | ever.

3 O ye *Heavens,* | bless · ye the | Lord : praise *Him,* and | magni - fy | Him · for | ever.

4 O ye *Waters* that be above the *firmament,* | bless · ye the | Lord : praise *Him,* and | magni - fy | Him · for | ever.

5 O all ye *Powers* of the *Lord,* | bless · ye the | Lord : praise *Him,* and | magni - fy | Him · for | ever.

6 O ye *Sun* and *Moon,* | bless · ye the | Lord : praise *Him,* and | magni - fy | Him · for | ever.

7 O ye *Stars* of *Heaven,* | bless · ye the | Lord : praise *Him,* and | magni - fy | Him · for | ever.

8 O ye *Showers* and *Dew,* | bless · ye the | Lord : praise *Him,* and | magni - fy | Him · for | ever.

9 O ye *Winds* of *God,* | bless · ye the | Lord : praise *Him,* and | magni - fy | Him · for | ever.

10 O ye *Fire* and *Heat,* | bless · ye the | Lord : praise *Him,* and | magni - fy | Him · for | ever.

11 O ye *Winter* and *Summer,* | bless · ye the | Lord : praise *Him,* and | magni - fy | Him · for | ever.

12 O ye *Dews* and *Frosts,* | bless · ye the | Lord : praise *Him,* and | magni - fy | Him · for | ever.

13 O ye *Frost* and *Cold,* | bless · ye the | Lord : praise *Him,* and | magni - fy | Him · for | ever.

14 O ye *Ice* and *Snow,* | bless · ye the | Lord : praise *Him,* and | magni - fy | Him · for | ever.

15 O ye *Nights* and *Days,* | bless · ye the | Lord : praise *Him,* and | magni - fy | Him · for | ever.

16 O ye *Light* and *Darkness,* | bless · ye the | Lord : praise *Him,* and | magni - fy | Him · for | ever.

17 O ye *Lightnings* and *Clouds,* | bless · ye the | Lord : praise *Him,* and | magni - fy | Him · for | ever.

MORNINGTON.

18 O let the *Earth* | bless · the | Lord : yea let it praise *Him,* and | magni - fy | Him · for | ever.

MORNING PRAYER.

19 O ye Mountains and *Hills,* | bless · ye the | Lord : praise *Him,* and | magni - fy | Him · for | ever.
20 O all ye Green Things upon the *earth,* | bless · ye the | Lord : praise *Him,* and | magni - fy | Him · for | ever.
21 O ye *Wells,* | bless · ye the | Lord : praise *Him,* and | magni - fy | Him · for | ever.
22 O ye Seas and *Floods,* | bless · ye the | Lord : praise *Him,* and | magni - fy | Him · for | ever.
23 O ye Whales, and all that move in the *waters,* | bless · ye the | Lord · praise *Him,* and | magni - fy | Him · for | ever.
24 O all ye Fowls of the *Air,* | bless · ye the | Lord : praise *Him,* and | magni - fy | Him · for | ever.
25 O all ye Beasts and *Cattle,* | bless · ye the | Lord : praise *Him,* and | magni - fy | Him · for | ever.

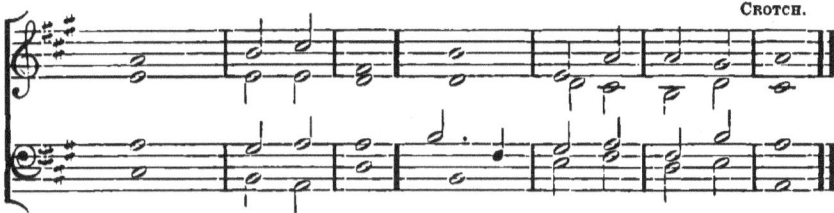

CROTCH.

26 O ye Children of *Men,* | bless · ye the | Lord : praise *Him,* and | magni - fy | Him · for | ever.
27 O let *Israel* | bless · the | Lord : praise *Him,* and | magni - fy | Him · for | ever.
28 O ye Priests of the *Lord,* | bless · ye the | Lord : praise *Him,* and | magni - fy | Him · for | ever.
29 O ye Servants of the *Lord,* | bless · ye the | Lord : praise *Him,* and | magni - fy | Him · for | ever.
30 O ye Spirits and Souls of the *Righteous,* | bless · ye the | Lord : praise *Him,* and | magni - fy | Him · for | ever.
31 O ye holy and humble Men of *heart,* | bless · ye the | Lord : praise *Him,* and | magni - fy | Him · for | ever. [GLORIA PATRI.]

Benedictus.

MORNING PRAYER. 9

Monk.

From Beethoven.

Benedictus.—St. Luke 1: 68.

B LESSED be the Lord *God* of | Is - ra- | el : for He hath *visited* | and · re- | deemed · His | people;

2 And hath raised up a mighty *salvation* | for · = | us : in the *house* | of · His | ser - vant | David;

3 As He spake by the *mouth* of His | ho - ly | Prophets : which have *been* | since · the | world · be- | gan.

4 That we should be saved *from* our | en - e- | mies : and *from* the | hand · of | all · that | hate us;

5 To perform the mercy *promised* to | our · fore- | fathers : and to *remember* His | ho - ly | co - ve- | nant;

6 To perform the oath which He sware to our *forefather* | A - bra- | ham : *that* | He · would | give · = | us;

7 That we being delivered out of the *hand* of our | en - e- | mies : might *serve* | Him · with- | out · = | fear;

8 In holiness and *righteousness* be- | fore · = | Him : *all* the | days · of | our · = | life.

9 And thou Child, shalt be called the *Prophet* | of · the | Highest : for thou shalt go before the face of the *Lord* | to · pre- | pare · His | ways;

10 To give knowledge of *salvation* | unto · His | people : *for* the re- | mis - sion | of · their | sins;

11 Through the tender *mercy* of | our · = | God : whereby the day-spring from on *high* | hath · = | visit - ed | us;

12 To give light to them that sit in darkness, and *in* the | shadow · of | death : and to guide our *feet* | in - to the | way · of | peace.

Glory be to the *Father*, | and · to the | Son : *and* | to · the | Ho - ly | Ghost;

As it was in the beginning, is *now*, and | ev - er | shall be : *world* with- | out · end | A · = | men.

Jubilate.

MORNING PRAYER.

Jubilate Deo.

Psalm 100.

O BE joyful in the *Lord,* | all · ye | lands : serve the Lord with gladness, and come before His | pre - sence | with · a | song.

2 Be ye sure that the *Lord,* | He · is | God : it is He that hath made us, and not we ourselves; we are His *people,* and the | sheep · of | His · = | pasture.

3 O go your way into His gates with thanksgiving, and *into* His | courts · with | praise : be thankful unto *Him,* and | speak · good | of · His | Name.

4 For the Lord is gracious, His *mercy* is | ev - er- | lasting : and His truth endureth from *generation* to | ge - ner- | a · = | tion.

GLORY be to the *Father,* | and · to the | Son : *and* | to · the | Ho - ly | Ghost:

As it was in the beginning, is *now,* and | ev - er | shall be : *world* with- | out · end | A · = | men.

Magnificat.

EVENING PRAYER.

Magnificat.—St. Luke 1: 46.

MY *soul* doth | magni - fy the | LORD : and my spirit hath *rejoiced* in | God · my | Sa · = | viour.

2 *For* He | hath · re- | garded : the *lowliness* of | His · hand- | maid · = | en.

3 For *behold* from | hence · = | forth : all *generations* shall | call · me | bless · = | ed.

4 For He that is *mighty* hath | magni - fied | me : *and* | ho - ly | is · His | Name.

*5 And His mercy is on *them* that | fear · = | Him : *throughout* | all · gener- | a · = | tions.

6 He hath showed *strength* | with · His | arm : He hath scattered the proud, in the *imagination* | of · = | their · = | hearts.

7 He hath put down the *mighty* | from · their | seat : and hath *exalted* the | hum - ble | and · = | meek.

8 He hath filled the *hungry* with | good · = | things : and the *rich* He | hath · sent | emp - ty a- | way.

9 He remembering His mercy, hath holpen His *servant* | Is - ra- | el : as He promised to our forefathers, *Abraham* | and · his | seed · for | ever.

GLORY be to the *Father* | and · to the | Son : *and* | to · the | Ho - ly | Ghost;

As it was in the beginning, is *now*, and | ev - er | shall be : *world* with- | out · end | A · = | men.

* *Repeat here second part of Double Chant.*

Cantate.

Cantate Domino.—Psalm 98.

O SING unto the *Lord* a | new • = | song : for *He* | hath • done | marvel - lous | things.

2 With His own right hand, and *with* His | ho - ly | arm : hath He *gotten* Him- | self • the | vic - to- | ry.

3 The Lord *declared* | His • sal- | vation : His righteousness hath He openly *showed* | in • the | sight • of the | heathen.

4 He hath remembered His mercy and truth *toward* the | house • of | Israel : and all the ends of the world have *seen* the sal- | va - tion | of • our | God.

5 Show yourselves joyful unto the *Lord* | all • ye | lands : *sing*, re- | joice • = | and • give | thanks.

6 Praise the *Lord* up- | on • the | harp : sing to the *harp* with a | psalm • of | thanks • = | giving.

7 With trumpets *also* | and • = | shawms : O show yourselves *joyful* be- | fore • the | Lord • the | King.

8 Let the sea make a noise, and *all* that | there - in | is : the round *world*, and | they • that | dwell • there- | in.

9 Let the floods clap their hands, and let the hills be joyful *together* be- | fore • the | Lord : *for* He | cometh • to | judge • the | earth.

10 With righteousness *shall* He | judge • the | world : and the *people* | with • = | e - qui- | ty.

GLORY be to the *Father*, | and • to the | Son : *and* | to • the | Ho - ly | Ghost;

As it was in the beginning, is *now*, and | ev - er | shall be : *world* with- | out • end | A • = | men.

Bonum est.

EVENING PRAYER.

Bonum est confiteri.

Psalm 92.

IT is a good thing to give *thanks* | un - to the | Lord : and to sing *praises* unto | Thy · Name | O · most | Highest;

2 To tell of Thy loving-kindness *early* | in · the | morning : and of Thy *truth* | in · the | night · = | season.

3 Upon an instrument of ten *strings*, and up- | on · the | lute : upon a loud *instru- ment*, | and · up- | on · the | harp.

4 For Thou Lord hast made me *glad* | through · Thy | works : and I will rejoice in giving praise *for* the oper- | a - tions | of · Thy | hands.

Glory be to the *Father*. | and · to the | Son : *and* | to · the | Ho - ly | Ghost;

As it was in the beginning, is *now*, and | ev - er | shall be : *world* with- | out · end | A · = | men.

Nunc dimitis.

EVENING PRAYER. 19

PRING.

GREGORIAN.

ROGERS.

Nunc dimittis.

St. Luke 2 : 29.

LORD, now lettest Thou Thy *servant* de- | part · in | peace : ac- | cord - ing | to ·
Thy | word.
 2 *For* mine | eyes · have | seen : *Thy* | = · sal- | va · = | tion.
 3 Which *Thou* | hast · pre- | pared : *before* the | face · of | all · = | people;
 4 To be a *light* to | lighten · the | Gentiles : and to be the glory of *Thy* | peo - ple |
Is - ra- | el.
 GLORY be to the *Father*, | and · to the | Son : *and* | to · the | Ho - ly | Ghost;
 As it was in the beginning, is *now* and | ev - er | sh all be : *world* with- | out · end |
A · = | men.

Deus misereatur.

EVENING PRAYER.

Deus misereatur.

Psalm 67.

G OD be merciful unto *us*, and | bless · = | us : and show us the light of his countenance, *and* be | merci - ful | un - to | us.

2 That Thy *way* may be | known up - on | earth : Thy *saving* | health · a- | mong · all | nations.

3 Let the people *praise* | Thee · O | God : yea let *all* the | peo - ple | praise · = | Thee.

4 O let the nations *rejoice* | and · be | glad : for Thou shalt judge the folk righteously, and *govern* the | na - tions up- | on · = | earth.

5 Let the people *praise* | Thee · O | God : yea let *all* the | peo - ple | praise · = | Thee.

6 Then shall the *earth* bring | forth · her | increase : and God, even our own *God*, shall | give · us | His · = | blessing.

7 *God* shall | bless · = | us : and all the ends of the *world* | shall · = | fear · = | Him.

Glory be to the *Father*, | and · to the | Son : *and* | to · the | Ho - ly | Ghost;

As it was in the beginning, is *now*, and | ev - er | shall be : *world* with- | out · end | A · = | men.

EVENING PRAYER. 23

Benedic, anima mea.

Psalm 103.

PRAISE the *Lord*, | O · my | soul : and all that is within *me* | praise · His | ho - ly | Name.

2 Praise the *Lord*, | O · my | soul : and forget *not* | all · His | ben - e- | fits;

3 Who *forgiveth* | all · thy | sin : and healeth *all* | thine · in- | firm - i- | ties;

4 Who saveth thy *life* | from · de- | struction : and crowneth *thee* with | mercy · and | lov - ing- | kindness.

5 O praise the Lord ye Angels of His, ye *that* ex- | cel · in | strength : ye that fulfil His commandment, and hearken *unto* the | voice · of | His · = | word.

6 O praise the *Lord*, all | ye · His | hosts : ye *servants* of | His · that | do · His | pleasure.

7 O speak good of the Lord, all ye works of His, in all *places* of | His · do- | minion : praise *thou* the | Lord · = | O · my | soul.

Glory be to the *Father*, | and · to the | Son : *and* | to · the | Ho - ly | Ghost;

As it was in the beginning, is *now*, and | ev - er | shall be : *world* with- | out · end | A · = | men.

PROPER ANTHEMS.

(IN PLACE OF VENITE.)

Easter Day.

CHRIST our Passover is *sacrificed* | for · = | us : *therefore* | let · us | keep · the | feast;

Not with the old leaven, neither with the leaven of *malice* and | wick - ed- | ness: but with the unleavened *bread* of sin- | cer - i- | ty · and | truth.   1 *Cor.* v. 7.

CHRIST being raised from the *dead*, | dieth · no | more : death hath no *more* do- | min - ion | o - ver | Him.

For in that He died, He *died* unto | sin · = | once : but in that He *liveth*, He | liv - eth | un - to | God.

Likewise reckon ye also yourselves to be dead *indeed* | un - to | sin : but alive unto *God* through | Je - sus | Christ · our | Lord.   *Rom.* vi. 9.

CHRIST is *risen* | from · the | dead : and *become* the | first - fruits of | them · that | slept.

For *since* by | man · came | death : by man came *also* the resur- | rec - tion | of · the | dead.

For as in *Adam* | all · = | die : even so in *Christ* shall | all · be | made · a- | live.   1 *Cor.* xv. 10.

GLORY be to the *Father*, | and · to the | Son : *and* | to · the | Ho - ly | Ghost;

As it was in the beginning, is *now*, and | ev - er | shall be : *world* with- | out · end. | A · = | men.

Thanksgiving-Day.

Elvey.

PRAISE ye the Lord; for it is good to sing *praises* | unto · our | God : for it is *pleasant*, | and · = | praise · is | comely.

2 The Lord doth build *up* Je- | ru - sa- | lem : He gathereth *together* the | out - casts of | Is - ra- | el.

3 He healeth those that *are* | broken · in | heart : *and* | bind - eth | up · their | wounds.

4 He covereth the heaven with clouds, and prepareth *rain* | for · the | earth : He maketh the *grass* to | grow · up- | on · the | mountains.

5 He giveth to the *beast* | his · = | food : and to the *young* | ra - vens | which · = | cry.

6 Praise the Lord, O Je- | ru - sa- | lem : *praise* | thy · God | O · = | Sion.

7 For He hath strengthened the *bars* | of · thy | gates : and hath *blessed* thy | chil - dren with- | in · = | thee.

8 He maketh *peace* | in · thy | borders : and filleth thee *with* the | fin - est | of · the | wheat.

Glory be to the *Father*, | and · to the | Son : *and* | to · the | Ho - ly | Ghost;

As it was in the beginning, is *now*, and | ev - er ¦ shall be : *world* with- | out · end. | A · = | men.

Consecration of Churches.

WOODWARD.

Psalm 24.—*Domini est terra.*

THE earth is the LORD's, and *all* that | there - in | is : the compass of the *world,* and | they · that | dwell · there- | in.

2 For He hath founded *it* up- | on · the | seas : *and* pre- | pared · it up- | on · the | floods.

3 Who shall ascend into the *hill* | of · the | LORD : or who shall rise *up* | in · His | ho - ly | place.

4 Even he that hath clean *hands,* and a | pure · = | heart : and that hath not lift up his mind unto *vanity,* nor | sworn · to de- | ceive · his | neighbour.

5 He shall receive the *blessing* | from · the | LORD : and righteousness *from* the | God · of | his · sal- | vation.

6 This is the generation of *them* that | seek · = | Him : even of *them* that | seek · thy | face · O | Jacob.

7 Lift up your heads O ye gates; and be ye lift up, ye *ever-* | last - ing | doors : and the *King* of | glo - ry | shall · come | in.

8 Who *is* the | King · of | glory : It is the LORD strong and mighty, *even* the | Lord · = | mighty · in | battle.

9 Lift up your heads O ye gates, and be ye lift up, ye *ever-* | last - ing | doors : and the *King* of | glo - ry | shall · come | in.

10 Who *is* the | King · of | glory : Even the LORD of *hosts,* | He · is the | King · of | glory.

Institution of Ministers.

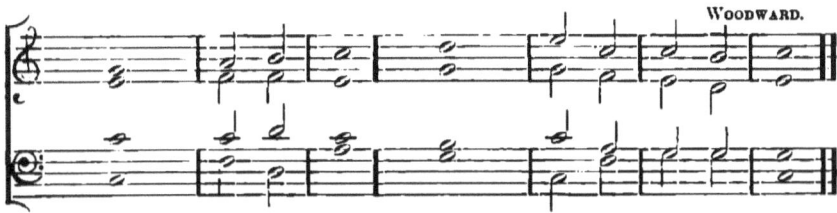

WOODWARD.

Laudate nomen.

O PRAISE the LORD, laud *ye* the | Name · of the | LORD : praise it O *ye* | serv - ants | of · the | LORD.

2 Ye that stand in the *house* | of · the | LORD : in the *courts* of the | house · of | our · = | God.

3 O praise the *Lord*, for the | Lord · is | gracious : O sing praises unto His *Name*, | for · = | it · is | lovely.

4 The LORD is *gracious* and | mer - ci- | ful : long-*suffering* | and · of | great · = | goodness.

5 The LORD is *loving* unto | eve - ry | man : and His *mercy* is | o - ver | all · His | works.

6 All Thy works *praise* | Thee · O | LORD : and Thy *saints* give | thanks · = | un - to | Thee.

7 The LORD doth build *up* Je- | ru - sa- | lem : and gather *together* the | out - casts of | Is - ra- | el.

8 He healeth those that *are* | broken · in | heart : and giveth *medicine* to | heal · = | their · = | sickness.

9 The LORD's delight is in *them* that | fear · = | Him : and *put* their | trust · in | His · = | mercy.

10 Praise the LORD, *O* Je- | ru - sa- | lem : *praise* | thy · God | O · = | Sion.

11 For He hath made fast the *bars* | of · thy | gates : and hath *blessed* thy | child - ren with- | in · = | thee.

12 He maketh *peace* | in · thy | borders : and filleth *thee* | with · the | flour · of | wheat.

13 He is our God, even the God of *whom* | cometh · sal- | vation : God is the *Lord*, by | whom · we es- | cape · = | death.

14 O God, wonderful art Thou in *Thy* | ho - ly | places : even the God of Israel, He will give strength and power unto His *people*. | Bless - ed | be · = | God.

GLORY be to the *Father*, | and · to the | Son : *and* | to · the | Ho - ly | Ghost;

As it was in the beginning, is *now*, and | ev - er | shall be : *world* with- | out · end. | A · = | men.

Burial of the Dead.

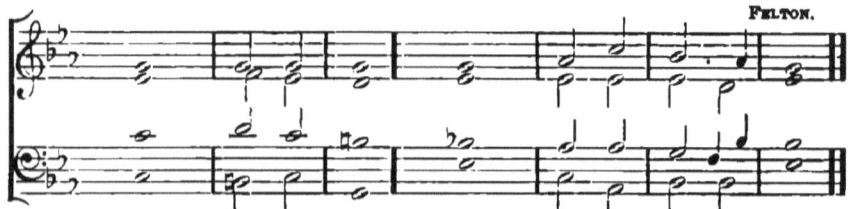
FELTON.

L ORD, let me know my end, and the *number* | of · my | days : that I may be *certified* how | long · I | have · to | live.

2 Behold, Thou hast made my days as it *were* a | span · = | long : and mine age is even as nothing in respect of Thee, and verily every man *living* is | al - to- | geth - er | vanity.

3 For man walketh in a vain shadow, and *disquieteth* him- | self · in | vain : he heapeth up riches, and cannot *tell* | who · shall | gath - er | them.

4 And now *Lord*, | what is · my | hope : *Truly* my | hope · is | even · in | Thee.

5 Deliver me from *all* | mine · of- | fences : and make me *not* a re- | buke · un- | to · the | foolish.

6 When Thou with rebukes dost chasten man for sin, Thou makest his beauty to consume away, like as it were a *moth* | fretting · a | garment : every man *therefore* | is · but | van - i- | ty.

7 Hear my prayer O LORD, and with Thine *ears* con- | sider · my | calling : hold *not* Thy | peace · = | at · my | tears :

8 For I am a | strang - er with | Thee : and a *sojourner,* as | all · my | fath - ers | were.

9 O spare me a little, that I *may* re- | cover · my | strength : before I go *hence,* | and · be | no · more | seen.

GOSS—BEETHOVEN.

10 *Lord,* Thou hast | been · our | refuge : from *one* gener- | a - tion | to · an- | other.

11 Before the mountains were brought forth, or ever the *earth* and the | world · were | made : Thou art God from *everlasting,* and | world · with- | out · = | end.

12 Thou turnest *man* | to · de- | struction : again Thou sayest, *Come* a- | gain, · ye | children · of | men.

13 For a thousand years in Thy *sight* are | but · as | yesterday : seeing that is *past* | as · a | watch · in the | night.

14 As soon as Thou scatterest them they are *even* | as · a | sleep : and fade *away* | sudden - ly | like · the | grass.

15 In the morning it is *green*, and | grow - eth | up : but in the evening it is cut *down*, | dri - ed | up · and | withered.

16 For we consume *away* in | Thy · dis- | pleasure : and are afraid *at* Thy | wrath - ful | in - dig- | nation.

17 Thou hast set our *misdeeds* be- | fore · = | Thee : and our secret *sins* in the | light of · Thy | coun - te- | nance.

18 For when Thou art angry, *all* our | days · are | gone : we bring our years to an *end*, as it | were · a | tale · that is | told.

19 The days of our age are threescore years and ten; and though men be so strong that they *come* to | four - score | years : yet is their strength then but labour and sorrow, so soon passeth *it* a- | way · and | we · are | gone.

20 So teach *us* to | number · our | days : that we *may* ap- | ply · our | hearts · unto | wisdom.

GLORY be to the *Father*, | and · to the | Son : *and* | to · the | Ho - ly | Ghost;

As it was in the beginning, is *now*, and | ev - er | shall be : *world* with- | out · end. | A · = | men.

Or this Chant, throughout.

MORLEY.

Gloria in Excelsis.

OLD CHANT.

GLORY *be* to | God · on | high : and on *earth,* | peace, · good | will · towards | men.

We praise Thee, we bless *Thee,* we | wor - ship | Thee : we glorify Thee, we give *thanks* to | Thee · for | Thy · great | glory.

O Lord *God,* | heaven - ly | King : *God* the | Fa - ther | al · = | mighty.

O Lord, the only begotten *Son* | Je - sus | Christ : O Lord God, *Lamb* of | God, · Son | of · the | Father.

That takest *away* the | sins · of the | world : have *mercy* | up - on | us.
Thou that takest *away* the | sins · of the | world : have *mercy* | up - on | us.
Thou that takest *away* the | sins · of the | world : re- | ceive · our | prayer.
Thou that sittest at the right *hand* of | God · the | Father : have *mercy* | up - on | us.

For Thou *only* | art · = | holy : *Thou* | on - ly | art · the | Lord.
Thou only O *Christ,* with the | Ho - ly | Ghost : art most *high* in the | glo - ry of | God · the | Father.

THE CHORAL SERVICE.

MORNING AND EVENING PRAYER.

Ferial.

THE CHORAL SERVICE. 33

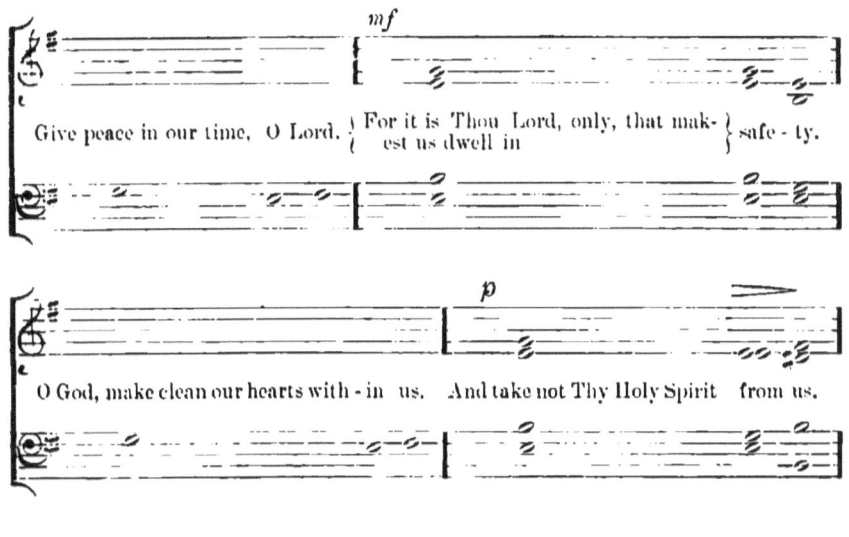

MORNING AND EVENING PRAYER.

Festal.

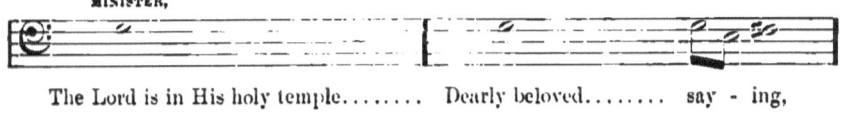

THE GENERAL CONFESSION.

Ely use. R. JANES. 1831.

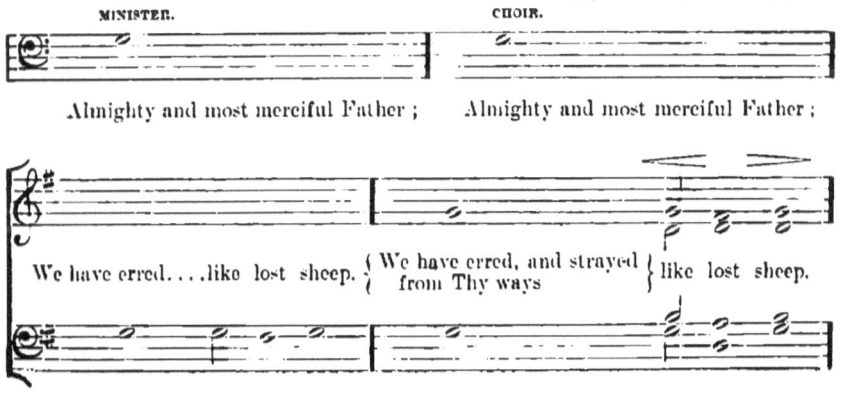

THE CHORAL SERVICE.   35

After the Absolution and Lord's Prayer.

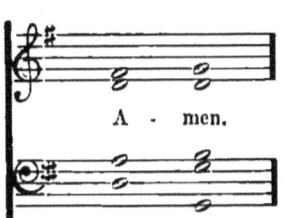

A - men.

T. TALLYS, about 1570.

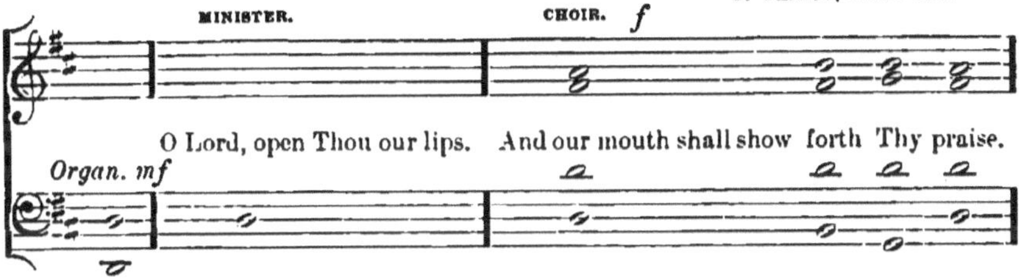

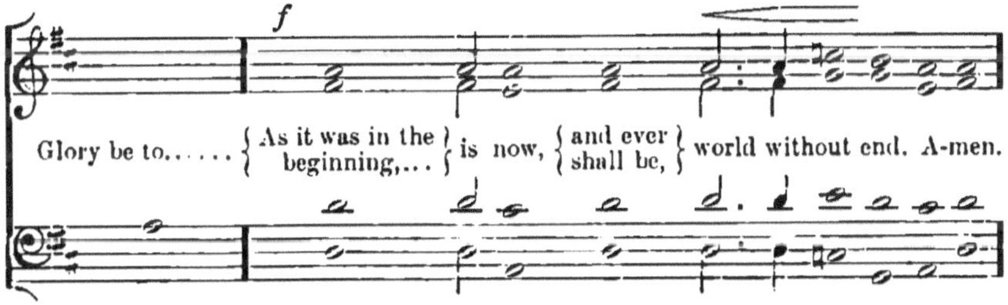

THE APOSTLES' CREED.

THE LITANY.

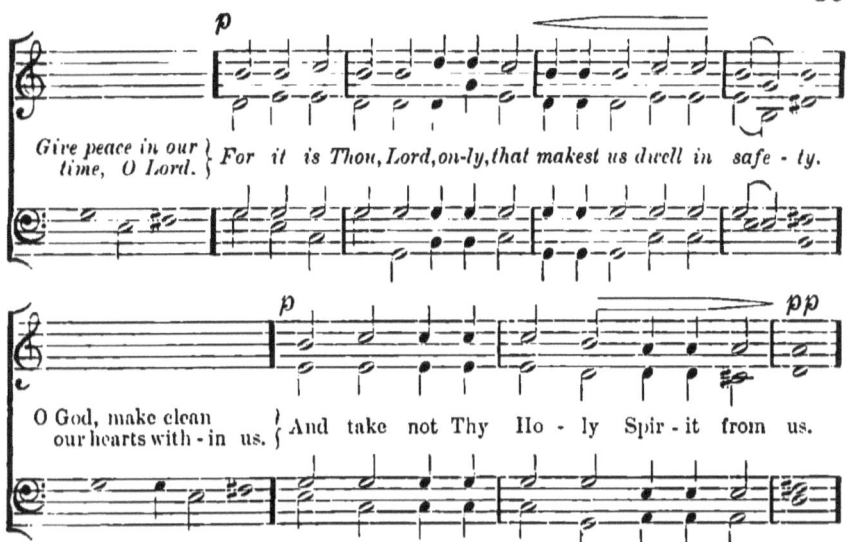

NOTE.—In these Responses, it is advisable for one or two first Basses to sing with the Tenors, in order to make the Plain-song duly prominent.

The Ferial Litany.

THE LITANY.

Remember not, Lord, our offences, nor the offences of our forefathers; neither take Thou vengeance of our sins; spare us, good Lord, spare Thy people, whom Thou hast redeemed with Thy most precious blood, and be not angry with .... us for ever : | *Spare us, good Lord.*

From all evil and mischief ; from sin ; from the crafts and assaults of the devil ; from Thy wrath, and from everlast - - - - - - - ing dam-nation : | *Good Lord, deliver us.*

From all blindness of heart ; from pride, vain-glory, and hypocrisy ; from envy, hatred, and malice, and all unchari- | ta-ble-ness :   *Good Lord, deliver us.*

From all inordinate and sinful affections ; and from all the deceits of the world, the flesh, | and the devil :   *Good Lord, deliver us.*

From lightning and tempest ; from plague, pestilence, and famine ; from battle and murder, and from | sud-den death :   *Good Lord, deliver us.*

From all sedition, privy conspiracy, and rebellion ; from all false doctrine, heresy, and schism ; from hardness of heart, and contempt of Thy Word | and Com-mandment :   *Good Lord, deliver us.*

By the mystery of Thy holy Incarnation : by Thy holy Nativity and Circumcision ; by Thy Baptism, Fasting, | and Tempt-ation.   *Good Lord, deliver us.*

By Thine Agony and Bloody Sweat ; by Thy Cross and Passion : by Thy precious Death and Burial ; by Thy glorious Resurrection and Ascension ; and by the coming of the | Ho-ly Ghost.   *Good Lord, deliver us.*

In all time of our tribulation ; in all time of our prosperity ; in the hour of death, and in the | day of judgment,   *Good Lord, deliver us.*

We sinners do beseech Thee to hear us, O Lord God ; and that it may please Thee to rule and govern Thy holy Church universal................. in the right way ; | *We beseech Thee to hear us, good Lord.*

That it may please Thee to bless and preserve all Christian Rulers and **Magistrates**, giving them grace to execute justice, and to | main-tain truth :   *We beseech Thee to hear us, good Lord.*

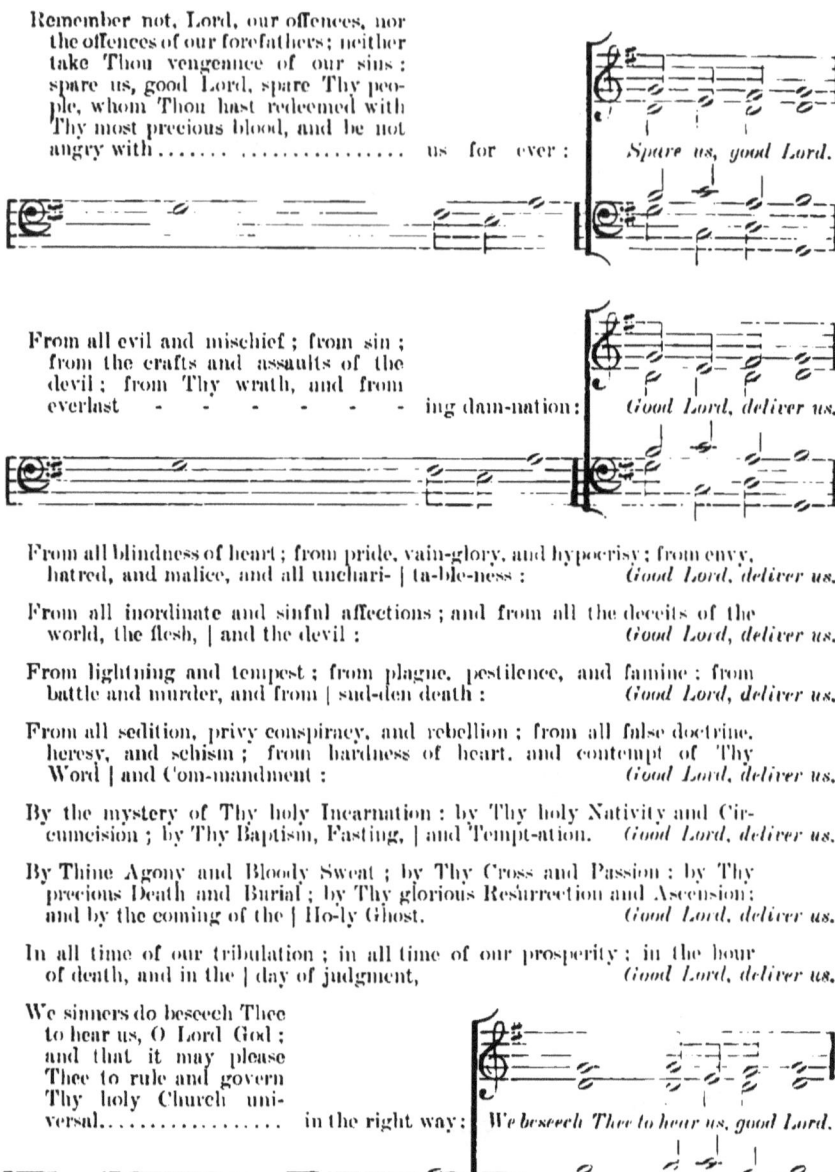

THE LITANY.

That it may please Thee to illuminate all Bishops, Priests, and Deacons, with true knowledge and understanding of Thy Word; and that both by their preaching and living they may set it forth, and show | it ac-cordingly;
We beseech Thee to hear us, good Lord.

That it may please Thee to send forth labourers | into Thine harvest;
We beseech Thee to hear us, good Lord.

That it may please Thee to bless and keep | all Thy people;
We beseech Thee to hear us, good Lord.

That it may please Thee to give to all nations unity, | peace, and concord;
We beseech Thee to hear us, good Lord.

That it may please Thee to give us an heart to love and fear Thee, and diligently to live after | Thy com-mandments; *We beseech Thee to hear us, good Lord.*

That it may please Thee to give to all Thy people increase of grace to hear meekly Thy Word, and to receive it with pure affection, and to bring forth the fruits | of the Spirit; *We beseech Thee to hear us, good Lord.*

That it may please Thee to bring into the way of truth all such as have erred, and | are de-ceived; *We beseech Thee to hear us, good Lord.*

That it may please Thee to strengthen such as do stand; and to comfort and help the weak-hearted; and to raise up those who fall; and finally to beat down Satan | under our feet; . *We beseech Thee to hear us, good Lord.*

That it may please Thee to succour, help, and comfort, all who are in danger, necessity and | trib-u-lation; *We beseech Thee to hear us, good Lord.*

That it may please Thee to preserve all who travel by land or by water, all women in the perils of childbirth, all sick persons, and young children; and to show Thy pity upon all prison- | ers and captives;
We beseech Thee to hear us, good Lord.

That it may please Thee to defend, and provide for, the fatherless children, and widows, and all who are desolate | and op-pressed;
We beseech Thee to hear us, good Lord.

That it may please Thee to have mercy up- | on — all men:
We beseech Thee to hear us, good Lord.

That it may please Thee to forgive our enemies, persecutors, and slanderers, and to | turn their hearts; *We beseech Thee to hear us, good Lord.*

That it may please Thee to give and preserve to our use the kindly fruits of the earth, so that in due time we | may en-joy them:
We beseech Thee to hear us, good Lord.

That it may please Thee to give us true repentance; to forgive us all our sins, negligences, and ignorances: and to endue us with the grace of Thy Holy Spirit to amend our lives according to Thy | ho-ly Word:
We beseech Thee to hear us, good Lord.

AFTER THE MINISTER.

Son of God, we beseech Thee to hear us.

THE LITANY.

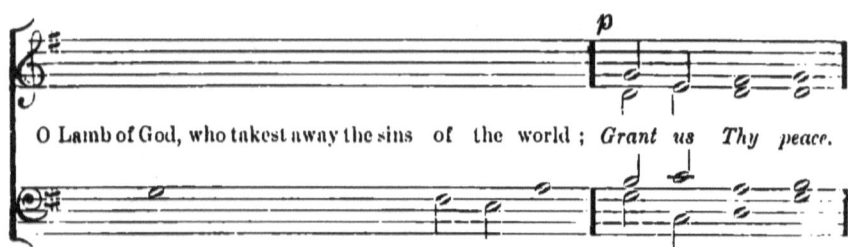

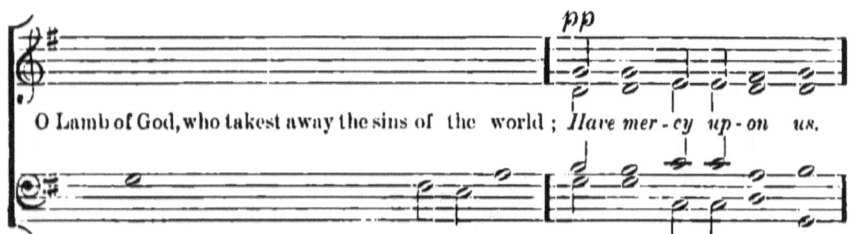

NOTE.—All that follows may be omitted, at discretion of Minister.

THE LITANY. 45

O God the Son, Re- | deemer ⋅ of the | world; ‖ have mercy upon us, | miserable | sin-ners.

O God the Holy Ghost, proceeding from the | Father ⋅ and the | Son; ‖ have mercy upon us, | miserable | sin-ners.

O holy, blessed, and glorious Trinity, three Persons | and ⋅ one | God; ‖ have mercy upon us, | miserable | sin-ners.

THE HOLY COMMUNION.

The Holy Communion.

KYRIE.

52 THE HOLY COMMUNION.

THE HOLY COMMUNION.

53

(9) J. T. FIELD.

Lord, have mer-cy up-on us, and in-cline our hearts to keep this law.

10. Lord, have mer-cy up-on us, and write all these Thy laws in our hearts, we be-seech.... Thee.

THE LESSER LITANY.

To be said if the Decalogue hath been omitted.

(1) T. TALLYS.

Lord, have mer-cy up-on us. Christ, have mer-cy up-on us.

Lord, have mer-cy up-on us.

(2) W. SMITHE.

Lord, have mer-cy up-on us.

THE HOLY COMMUNION.

Christ, have mer-cy up-on us. Lord, have mer-cy up-on us.

GLORIA TIBI.

(1) Tallys. — Glo-ry be to Thee, O Lord.
(2) Glo-ry be to Thee, O Lord.
(3) S. Reay. — Glo-ry be to Thee, O Lord.
(4) K. Hall. — Glo-ry be to Thee, O Lord.
(5) G. F. Cobb. — Glo-ry be to Thee, O Lord.
(6) Dr. Elvey. — Glo-ry be to Thee, O Lord.

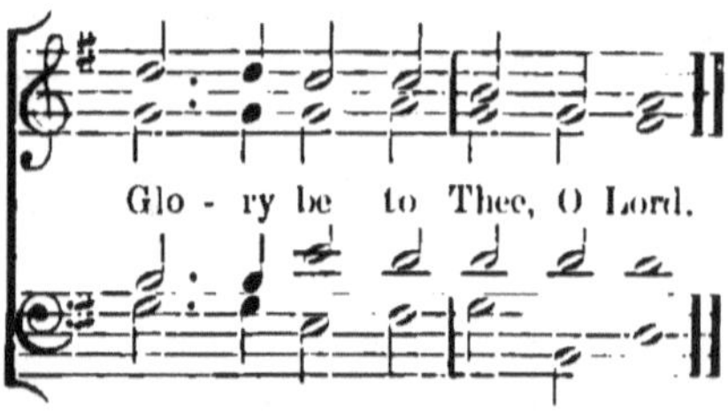

THE HOLY COMMUNION.

THE HOLY COMMUNION.

THE HOLY COMMUNION.

THE HOLY COMMUNION. 61

THE HOLY COMMUNION. 63

THE HOLY COMMUNION.

THE HOLY COMMUNION.

73

74   THE HOLY COMMUNION.

(5)

SOPRANOS (or TENORS.)   Dr. MARTIN.

THE HOLY COMMUNION.

(6)   Dr. Martin.

82 THE HOLY COMMUNION.

86 THE HOLY COMMUNION.

Organ with Voices.

(1) Benedictus.

SOPRANO. ♩ = 72.   C. GOUNOD.

pp Bless-ed is He.... who com-eth in.... the name of...

ALTO.

TENORS. *pp* Bless-ed is He.... who com-eth in.... the name of...

BASSES. *pp*

* This may be sung as Soprano Solo, as far as A ; to be followed by the entire movement in Chorus.

THE HOLY COMMUNION. 87

THE HOLY COMMUNION.

ff
rall.
Ho - san - na in the High - - - - - - est!
ff
rall.
f
cres. e rall.
a tempo.
ff

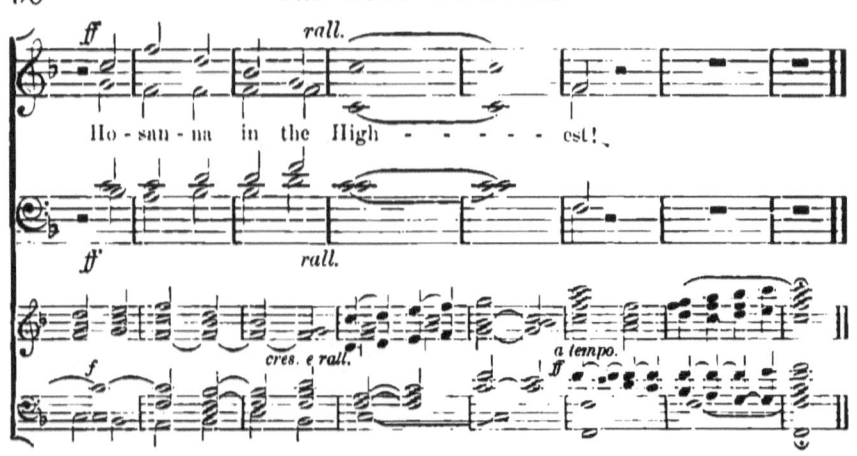

Agnus Dei.

(1)

J. B. Calkin.

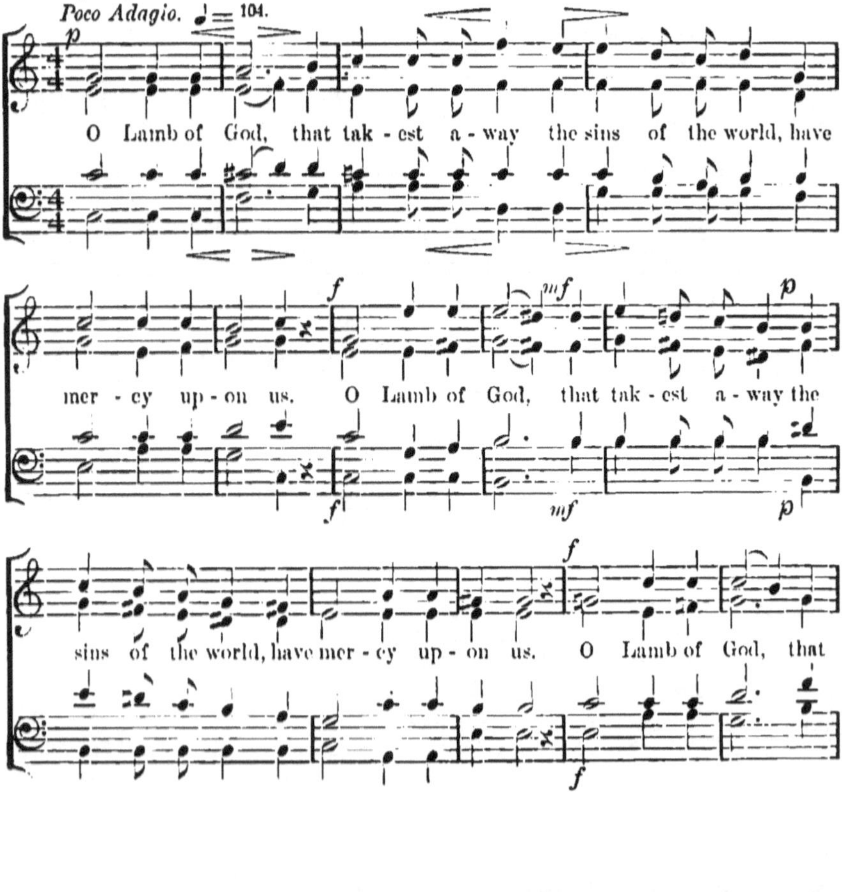
Poco Adagio. = 104.
p
O Lamb of God, that tak - est a - way the sins of the world, have
f
mf
p
mer - cy up - on us. O Lamb of God, that tak - est a - way the
f
mf
p
f
sins of the world, have mer - cy up - on us. O Lamb of God, that
f

THE HOLY COMMUNION.   91

96   THE HOLY COMMUNION.

NOTE.—This arrangement may be simplified by repeating sixteen bars from A to B, and omitting sixteen bars from B to C; also by taking four bars at C as Treble Solo, four bars at D as Tenor Solo, four bars at E as Solo or Duet, and by ending at F. The original arrangement is for two Tenors and two Basses throughout.

(1)   **The Lord's Prayer.**   MERBECKE—STAINER.

Our Fa-ther, Who art in heaven, Hal-low-ed be Thy Name: Thy kingdom come,

THE HOLY COMMUNION. 99

100 THE HOLY COMMUNION.

Gloria in Excelsis.

Dr. STEGGALL.

THE HOLY COMMUNION. 101

THE HOLY COMMUNION.

THE HOLY COMMUNION.

THE HOLY COMMUNION.

109

(2) Nicene Creed.

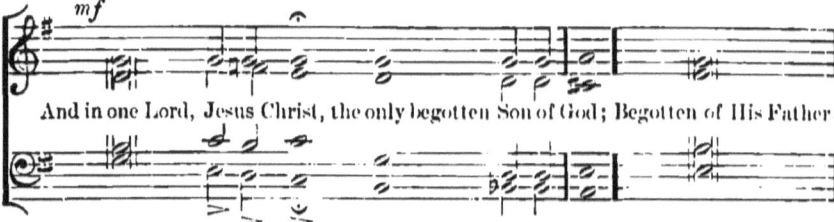

THE HOLY COMMUNION.

112   THE HOLY COMMUNION.

In harmony.

(1)   OFFERTORY SENTENCES.   From MERBECKE.

THE HOLY COMMUNION.

There-fore with Angels and Arch-an-gels, and with all the company of heav'n, we laud and magnify Thy glorious Name; ev-ermore praising Thee, and say-ing,

CHOIR. *Unison.* p   cres.

Ho-ly, Ho-ly, Ho-ly, Lord God of hosts, heaven and earth are full of Thy glo-ry: Glo-ry be to Thee, O Lord Most High. A-men.

Proper Prefaces.

UPON CHRISTMAS DAY, AND SEVEN DAYS AFTER.

Because Thou didst give Je-sus Christ, Thine on-ly Son, to be born

PRIEST.

THE HOLY COMMUNION.

as at this time.... for us; Who, by the operation of the Holy Ghost was made very man, of the substance of the Virgin Mary, His mother; and that without spot of sin, to make us clean from.... all sin. Therefore with Angels, etc.

UPON EASTER DAY, AND SEVEN DAYS AFTER.

But chiefly are we bound to praise Thee for the glorious Resurrection

PRIEST.

THE HOLY COMMUNION.

of Thy Son, Je - sus Christ our Lord; for He is the ve - ry Pas - chal Lamb, which was of - fer - ed for us, and hath tak - en a - way the sin of the world; Who by His death hath de-stroy-ed death, and, by His rising to life again, hath restored to us ev - er - last-ing life,

Therefore, etc.

UPON ASCENSION DAY, AND SEVEN DAYS AFTER.

Through Thy most dear - ly be - lov - ed Son, Je - sus Christ our Lord;

120 THE HOLY COMMUNION.

UPON WHITSUN-DAY, AND SIX DAYS AFTER.

Through Je - sus Christ.... our Lord; ac-cording to whose most true promise, the Holy Ghost came down as at this time from heaven, with a sudden great sound, as it had been a might - y wind, in the likeness of fiery tongues, lighting upon the Apostles, to teach them, and to lead them to.... all truth; giv-ing them both the gift of di - vers lan - guag - es,

Agnus Dei.

MERBECKE—STAINER.

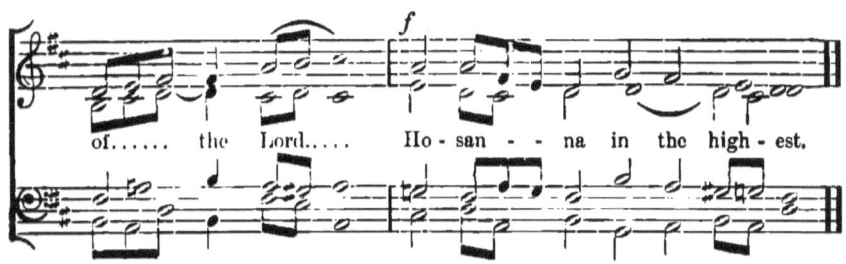

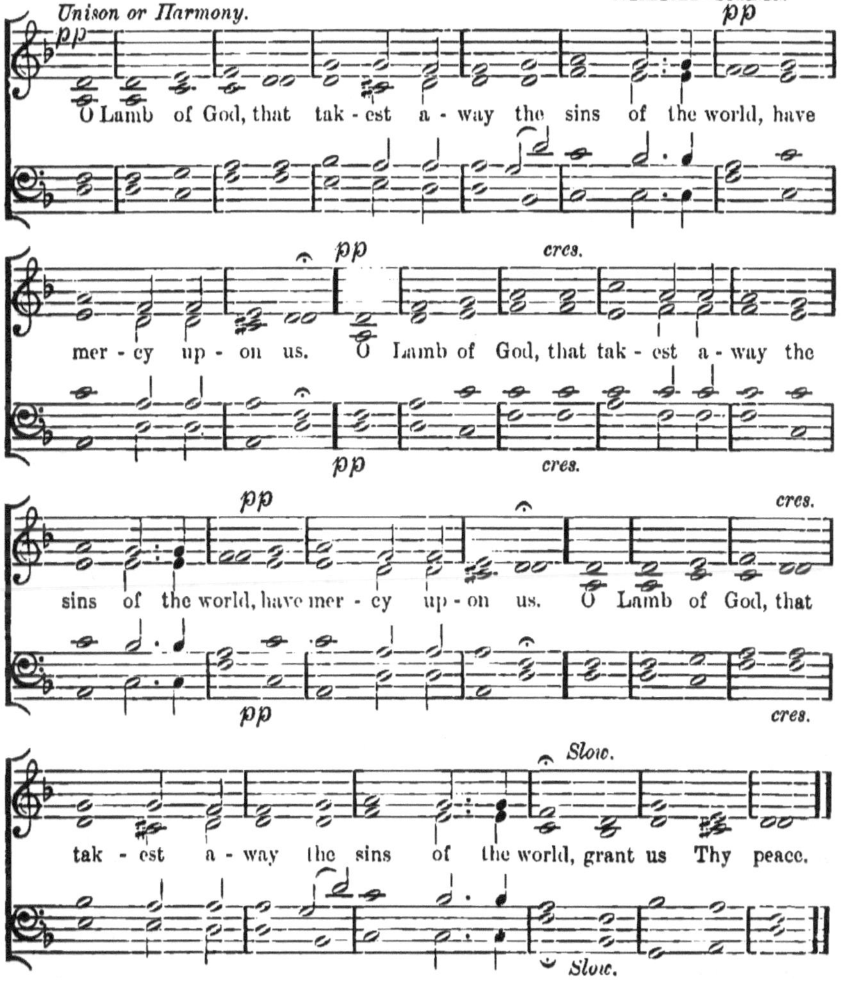

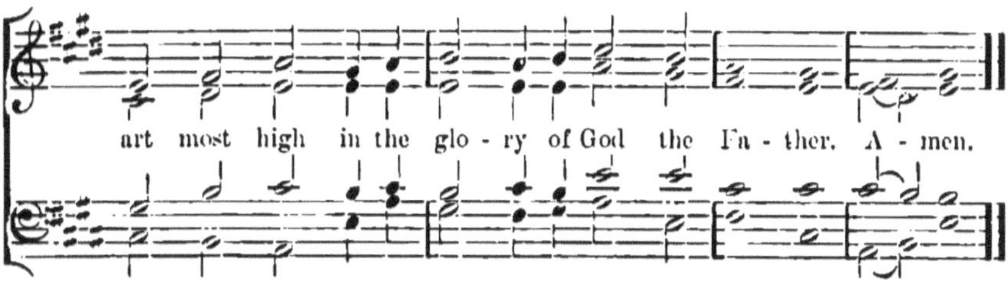
art most high in the glo - ry of God the Fa - ther. A - men.

THE CANTICLES AS ANTHEMS.

Te Deum laudamus.

J. B. CALKIN.

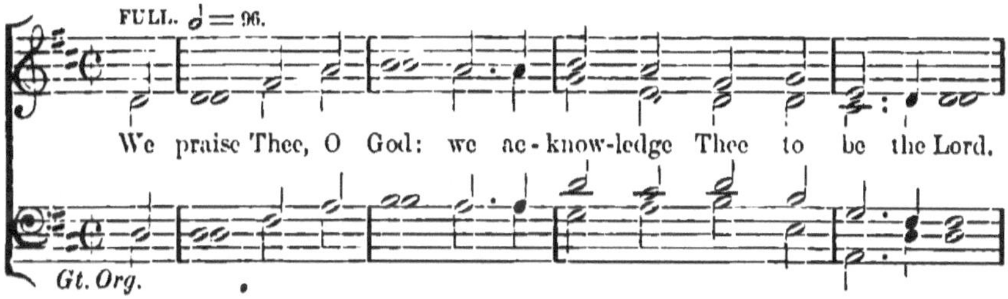
FULL. 𝅗𝅥 = 96.
We praise Thee, O God: we ac - know-ledge Thee to be the Lord.
Gt. Org.

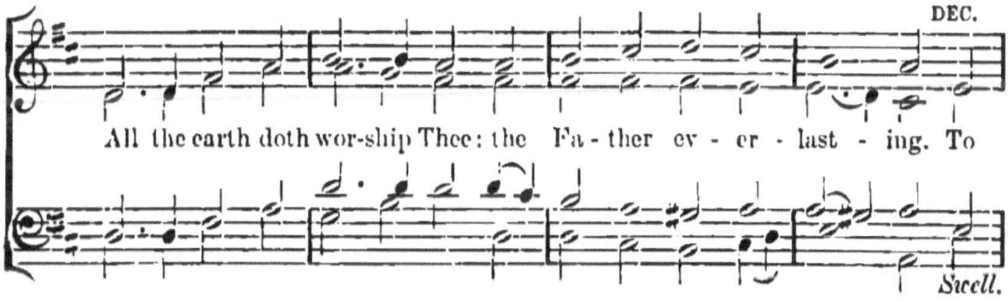
DEC.
All the earth doth wor-ship Thee: the Fa - ther ev - er - last - ing. To
Swell.

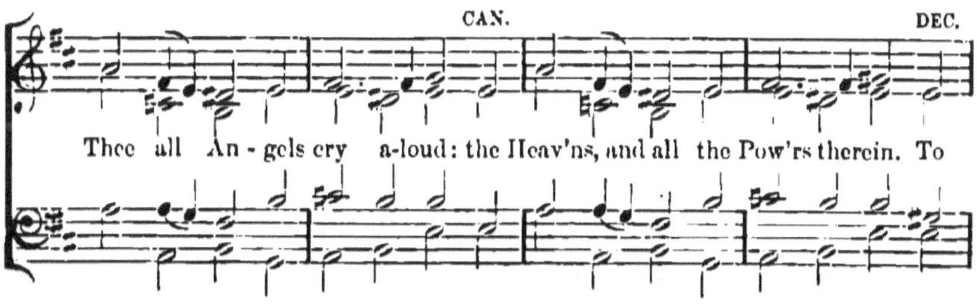
CAN.
DEC.
Thee all An - gels cry a-loud: the Heav'ns, and all the Pow'rs therein. To

* The Gloria Patri may follow here, except in Advent.

140 THE CANTICLES AS ANTHEMS.

Jubilate Deo.

J. B. CALKIN.

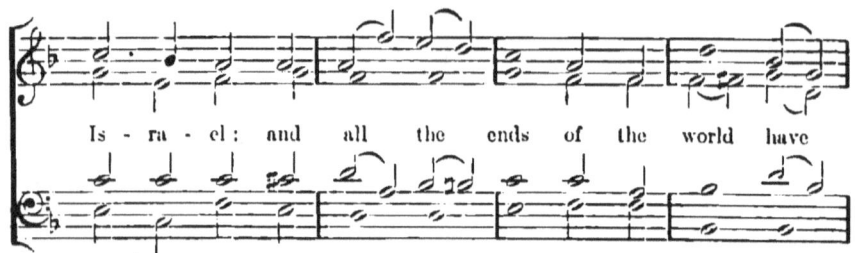

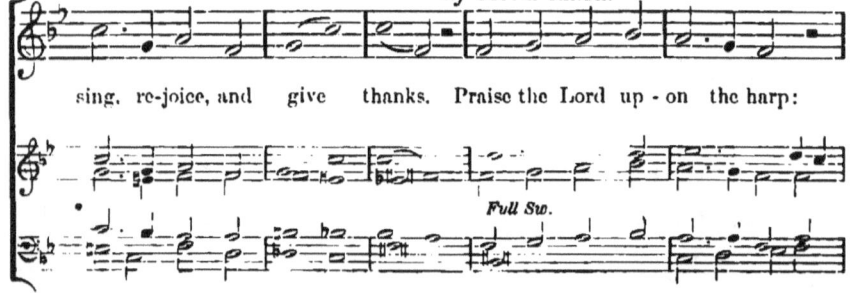

THE CANTICLES AS ANTHEMS. 149

Nunc dimittis.

C. H. Lloyd.

THE CANTICLES AS ANTHEMS.

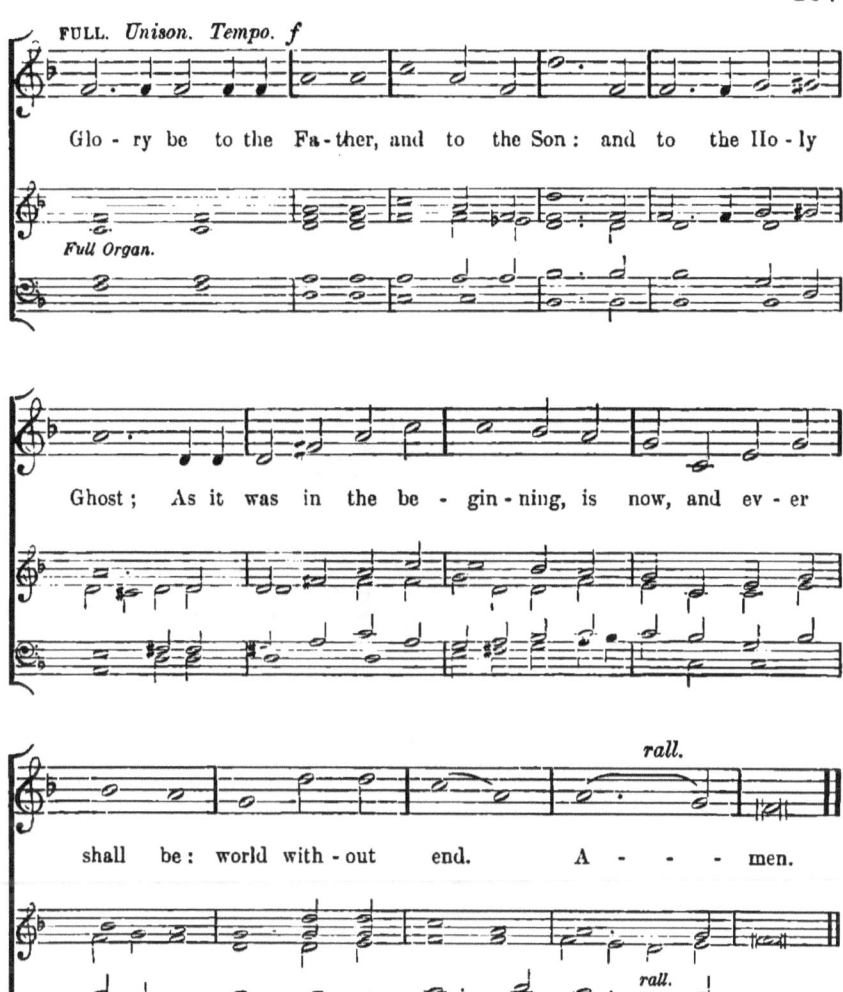

160   THE BURIAL SERVICE.

THE BURIAL SERVICE.

Continuation by H. PURCELL.

THE BURIAL SERVICE.
WITH PLAINSONG.

THE BURIAL SERVICE, WITH PLAINSONG.

THE ANTHEM.

Lord —, | let me know my end, and the *number* of my days : that I may be certified how *long* I have to live.

Behold, Thou hast made my days as it *were* a span long : and mine age is even as nothing in respect of Thee ; and verily every man living is *altogether* vanity.

For man walketh in a vain shadow, and disquieteth *himself* in vain : he heapeth up riches, and cannot tell *who* shall gather them.

And now, Lord, what is *my* hope : Truly my *hope* is even in Thee.

Deliver me from all *mine* offences : and make me not a rebuke *un* the fool — ish.

When Thou with rebukes dost chasten man for sin, Thou makest his beauty to consume away, like as it were a moth *fretting* a garment : every man therefore is *but* vanity.

Hear my prayer, O Lord, and with Thine ears *consider* my calling : hold not Thy *peace* at my tears :

For I am a *stranger* with Thee : and a sojourner, as *all* my fathers were.

O spare me a little, that I may *recover* my strength : before I go *hence*, and be no more seen.

Lord —, | Thou hast *been* our refuge : from one *generation* to anoth —er.

Before the mountains were brought forth, or ever the earth and the *world* were made : Thou art God from everlasting, and *world* without — end,

THE BURIAL SERVICE, WITH PLAINSONG. 165

Thou turnest *man* to destruction : again Thou sayest, Come *again*, ye children of men.

For a thousand years in Thy sight are *but* as yesterday : seeing that is past as a *watch* in the night.

As soon as Thou scatterest them they are even *as* a sleep : and fade away *suddenly* like the grass.

In the morning it is green, and *groweth* up : but in the evening it is cut down, dried *up*, and withered.

For we consume away in *Thy* displeasure : and are afraid at Thy *wrathful* indignation.

Thou hast set our *misdeeds* before Thee : and our secret sins in the light of *Thy* countenance.

For when Thou art angry all our *days* are gone : we bring our years to an end, as it *were* a tale that is told.

The days of our age are threescore years and ten ; and though men be so strong that they come to *fourscore* years : yet is their strength then but labour and sorrow ; so soon passeth it *away*, and we are gone.

So teach us to *number* our days : that we may apply our *hearts* unto wis — dom.

Glory be to the Father, *and* to the Son : *and* to the Holy Ghost ;

As it was in the beginning, is now, and *ever* shall be : world without end. A — men.

AFTER THE LESSON.

THE CANTICLES.
SET TO GREGORIAN TONES, WITH VARIED HARMONIES.
Venite

THE CANTICLES, SET TO GREGORIAN TONES. 169

Venite, exultemus Domino.

O — | come, let us *sing* un-to the Lord — : let us heartily *rejoice* in the strength of our salvation.

Let us come before his *presence* with thanks — giving : and show *ourselves* glad in Him with psalms — .

For the *Lord* is a great — God — : and a great *King* a-bove — all — gods — .

In His hand are all the *corners* of the earth — : and the *strength* of the hills is His — also.

The sea is *His*, and He made it : and His *hands* prepared the dry — land — .

O come, let us *worship* and fall down — : and *kneel* before the Lord our Maker.

For *He* is the Lord our God — : and we are the people of His pasture, *and* the sheep of His — hand — .

O worship the *Lord* in the beauty of holi-ness : let the whole *earth* stand in awe of Him — .

For He cometh, for He *cometh* to judge the earth — : and with right-eousness to judge the *world*, and the people with His truth — .

Glo - ry | be to the *Father*, and to the Son — : *and* to the Holy Ghost — :

As it | was in the beginning, is *now*, and ever shall be : *world* with-out end. A — men — .

Te Deum.

Te Deum laudamus.

We — | *praise* Thee, O God : we *acknowledge* Thee to be the Lord.
All the *earth* doth worship Thee : the *Father* everlast — ing.
To Thee all *Angels* cry aloud : the *Heavens* and all the Powers therein.
To Thee *Cherubim* and Seraphim : continually do cry,
Holy, Holy, Holy : *Lord* God of Sabaoth ;
Heaven and earth are *full* of the Majesty : *of* Thy — Glo — ry.
The glorious *company* of the Apostles : * praise — — — Thee.
The goodly *fellowship* of the Prophets : * praise — — — Thee.
The *noble* army of Martyrs : * praise — — — Thee.
The holy *Church* throughout all the world : * doth acknowledge Thee ;
The Fa — ther : *of* an infinite Majesty ;
Thine adorable true : * and — only Son ;
Also the Holy Ghost : *the* Com — — forter.
Thou *art* the King of Glory : * O — — — Christ.
Thou art the *everlasting* Son : * of the Fa — ther.
When Thou tookest upon *Thee* to deliver man : Thou didst humble
    Thyself to be born of a Vir — gin.
When Thou hadst *overcome* the sharpness of death : Thou didst open
    the Kingdom of *Heaven* to all believ — ers.
Thou sittest at the *right* hand of God : in the *Glory* of the Fa — ther.
We *believe* that Thou shalt come : *to* be — our — Judge.
We therefore pray *Thee*, help Thy servants : whom Thou hast *redeemed*
    with Thy precious blood.
Make them to be *numbered* with Thy Saints : in *glory* everlast — ing.
O *Lord*, save Thy people : *and* bless Thine heritage.
Govern — them : and *lift* them up for ev — er.
Day by — day : *we* magnify — Thee ;
And we *worship* Thy — Name : *ever*, world without — end.
Vouchsafe, O — Lord : to keep *us* this day without — sin.
O *Lord*, have mercy upon us : *have* mercy upon — us.
O Lord, let Thy *mercy* be upon us : *as* our trust is in — Thee.
O Lord, in *Thee* have I trusted : let me *never* be confound — ed.

* Omit the Reciting Note.

THE CANTICLES, SET TO GREGORIAN TONES.

THE CANTICLES, SET TO GREGORIAN TONES.

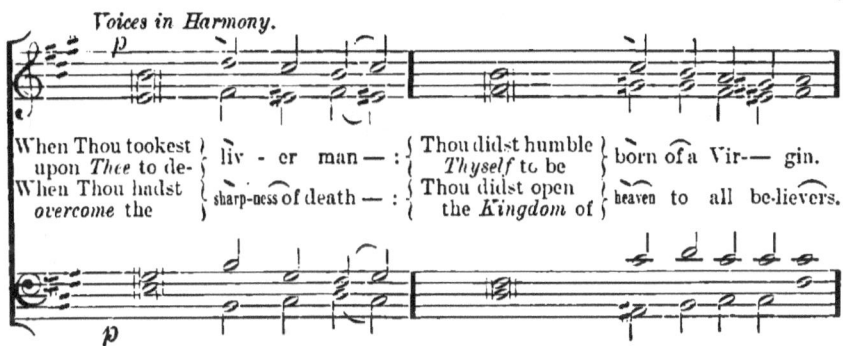

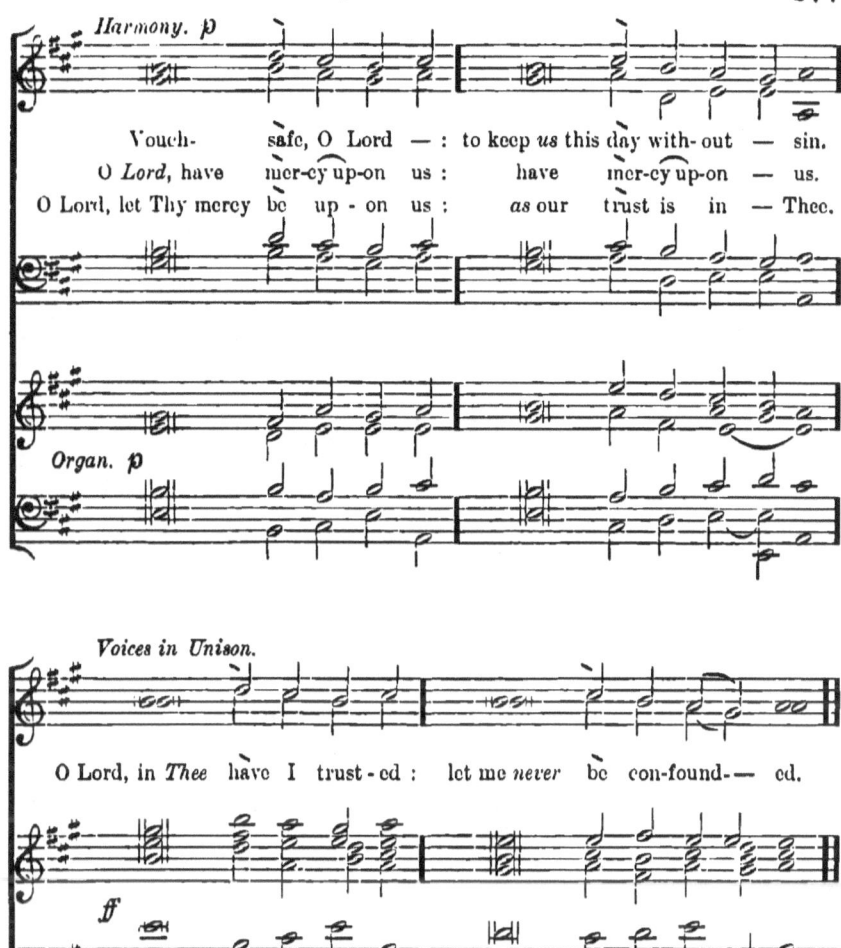

THE CANTICLES, SET TO GREGORIAN TONES.

Benedicite, omnia opera Domini.

O — | all ye Works of the Lord, bless ye the Lord — : praise *Him,* and magnify Him for ever.
O ye Angels of the Lord, bless ye the Lord — : praise *Him,* &c.
O ye Heavens, bless ye the Lord — : praise *Him,* &c.
O ye Waters that be above the firmament, bless ye the Lord — : praise, &c.
O all ye Powers of the Lord, bless ye the Lord — : praise *Him,* &c.
O ye Sun and Moon, bless ye the Lord — : praise *Him,* &c.
O ye Stars of Heaven, bless ye the Lord — : praise *Him,* &c.
O ye Showers and Dew, bless ye the Lord — : praise *Him,* &c.
O ye Winds of God, bless ye the Lord — : praise *Him,* &c.
O ye Fire and Heat, bless ye the Lord — : praise *Him,* &c.
O ye Winter and Summer, bless ye the Lord — : praise *Him,* &c.
O ye Dews and Frosts, bless ye the Lord — : praise *Him,* &c.
O ye Frost and Cold, bless ye the Lord — : praise *Him,* &c.
O ye Ice and Snow, bless ye the Lord — : praise *Him,* &c.
O ye Nights and Days, bless ye the Lord — : praise *Him,* &c.
O ye Light and Darkness, bless ye the Lord — : praise *Him,* &c.
O ye Lightnings and Clouds, bless ye the Lord — : praise *Him,* &c.
O let the Earth bless the Lord — : yea, let it praise *Him,* &c.
O ye Mountains and Hills, bless ye the Lord — : praise *Him,* &c.
O all ye Green Things upon the earth, bless ye the Lord — : praise, &c.
O ye Wells, bless ye the Lord — : praise *Him,* &c.
O ye Seas and Floods, bless ye the Lord — : praise *Him,* &c.
O ye Whales, and all that move in the waters, bless ye the Lord — : praise *Him,* &c.
O all ye Fowls of the Air, bless ye the Lord — : praise *Him,* &c.
O all ye Beasts and Cattle, bless ye the Lord — : praise *Him,* &c.
O ye Children of Men, bless ye the Lord — : praise *Him,* &c.
O let Israel bless the Lord — : praise *Him,* &c.
O ye Priests of the Lord, bless ye the Lord — : praise *Him,* &c.
O ye Servants of the Lord, bless ye the Lord — : praise *Him,* &c.
O ye Spirits and Souls of the Righteous, bless ye the Lord — : praise, &c.
O ye holy and humble Men of Heart, bless ye the Lord — : praise, &c.
Glo-ry | be to the *Father,* and to the Son — : *and* to the Holy Ghost —;
As it | was in the beginning, is *now,* and ever shall be : *world* without end. A — men —.

(3) **Benedicite.**

From Dr. GAUNTLETT.

3. O ye | Heavens, bless....
4. O ye | Waters that be above the firmament, bless....
5. O all ye | Powers of the Lord, bless..
6. O ye | Sun and Moon, bless...
7. O ye | Stars of Heaven, bless....
8. O ye | Showers and Dew, bless....
9. O ye | Winds of God, bless....
10. O ye | Fire and Heat, bless....
11. O ye | Winter and Summer, bless...
12. O ye | Dews and Frosts, bless....
13. O ye | Frost and Cold, bless....
14. O ye | Ice and Snow, bless...
15. O ye | Nights and Days, bless....
16. O ye | Light and Darkness, bless....
17. O ye | Lightnings and Clouds, bless..

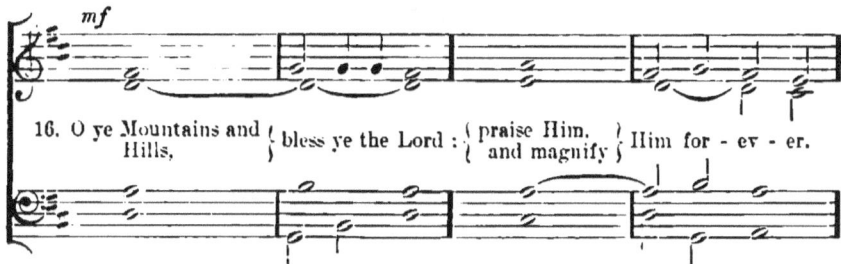

16. O ye Mountains and Hills, bless ye the Lord : praise Him, and magnify Him for - ev - er.

20. O all ye Green Things upon the earth, bless....
21. O ye Wells, bless....
22. O ye Seas and Floods, bless....
23. O ye Whales, and all that move in the waters, bless....
24. O all ye Fowls of the Air, bless....
25. O all ye Beasts and Cattle, bless....

26. O ye Children of Men, bless — ye the Lord —: praise Him, and magnify Him for ev - er.

27. O let | Israel bless —— the Lord — : praise....
28. O ye | Priests of the Lord, bless - ye....
29. O ye Servants of the Lord, bless - ye....
30. O ye | Spirits and Souls of the righteous, bless — ye....
31. O ye | holy and humble Men of heart, bless — ye....

Glo-ry be to the Father, and to the Son -: and to the Ho-ly Ghost -:
As it was in the beginning, is now, and ev - er shall be : world with-out end. A- — men —.

Benedictus.

Benedictus.—St. Luke 1 : 68.

Blessed | be the *Lord* God of Israel : for He hath *visited*, and redeemed
His people ;
And hath | raised up a *mighty* salvation for us : in the *house* of His
servant David ;
As He | spake by the *mouth* of His holy Prophets : which have *been*
since the world began — ;
That we | should be *saved* from our enemies : and *from* the hand of all
that hate us.

To per | form the mercy *promised* to our forefathers : and to *remember*
His — holy Covenant ;
To per | form the oath which He sware to our *forefather* Abraham :
that He would give — us — ;
That — | we being delivered out of the *hand* of our — enemies : *might*
serve Him without — fear — ;
In — | holiness and *righteousness* before — Him : *all* the days of our —
life — .
And thou, | child, shalt be called the *Prophet* of the Highest : for thou
shalt go before the face of the *Lord* to prepare His ways — ;
To give | knowledge of *salvation* unto His people : *for* the remission of
their — sins — ,
Through the | tender *mercy* of our — God : whereby the day-spring
from on *high* hath — visited us — ;
To give | light to them that sit in darkness, and *in* the shadow of death :
and to guide our *feet* into the way of peace — .
Glo - ry | be to the *Father*, and to the Son : *and* to the Holy Ghost — ;
As it | was in the beginning, is *now*, and ever shall be : world without
end. A — — — men — .

THE CANTICLES, SET TO GREGORIAN TONES.

Jubilate.

THE CANTICLES, SET TO GREGORIAN TONES. 189

Jubilate Deo.—Psalm c.

O be | joyful in the *Lord,* all ye lands : serve the LORD with gladness, and come *before* His presence with a song.

Be ye sure that the *Lord* He is God : it is He that hath made us, and not we ourselves ; we are His *people,* and the sheep of His pas — ture.

O go your way into His gates with thanksgiving, and into His *courts* with praise : be thankful unto Him, and *speak* good of His — Name.

For the LORD is gracious, His mercy is *everlasting* ; and His truth endureth from *generation* to genera — tion.

Glo - ry | be to the Father, *and* to the Son : *and* to the Holy Ghost ;

As it | was in the beginning, is *now,* and ever shall be : *world* without end. A — men.

THE CANTICLES, SET TO GREGORIAN TONES.

Magnificat.

Magnificat.—St. Luke 1 : 46.

My — | *soul* doth magnify the Lord : and my spirit hath *rejoiced* in God my Saviour.

For — | *He* hath regarded : the *lowliness* of His handmaiden.

For be- | *hold*, from hence — forth — : all *generations* shall call me blessed.

For — | He that is *mighty* hath magnified me : and *holy* is His Name —.

And His | *mercy* is on them that fear Him : *throughout* all generations.

He hath | showed *strength* with His arm — : He hath scattered the proud in the *imagination* of their hearts —.

He hath | put down the *mighty* from their seat — : and hath *exalted* the humble and meek —.

He hath | filled the *hungry* with good — things — : and the rich He hath *sent* empty away —.

He re- | membering His mercy hath *holpen* His servant Israel : as He promised to our forefathers, *Abraham* and his seed, for ever.

Glo-ry | be to the *Father*, and to the Son — : *and* to the Holy Ghost —;

As it | was in the beginning, is *now*, and ever shall be : world without end. A — men —.

(4) Magnificat.

Arranged by G. H. GREGORY.

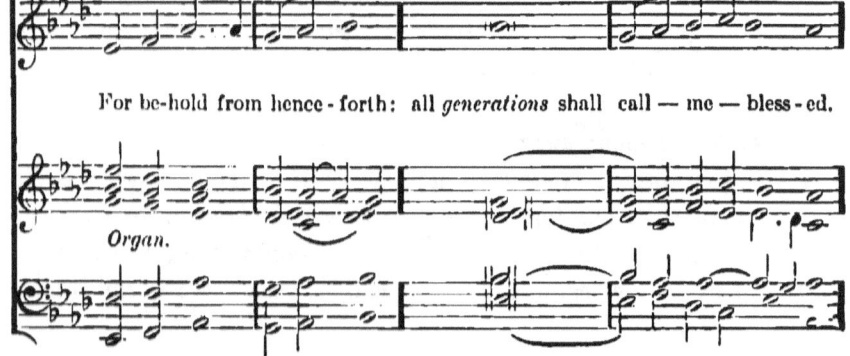

THE CANTICLES, SET TO GREGORIAN TONES. 193

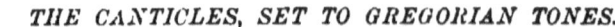

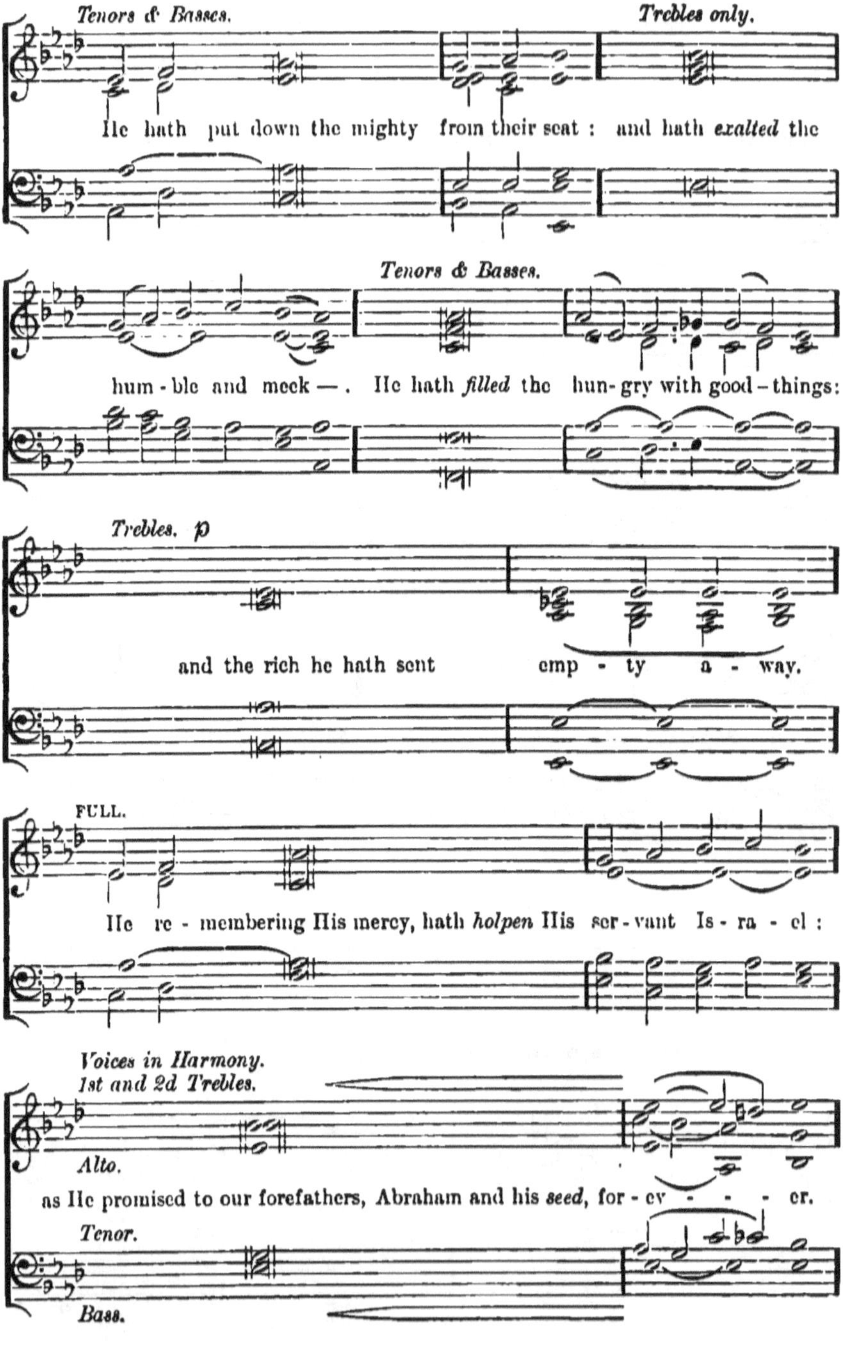

Tenors & Basses.
Trebles only.
He hath put down the mighty from their seat : and hath exalted the
Tenors & Basses.
hum - ble and meek — . He hath filled the hun- gry with good – things:
Trebles. p
and the rich he hath sent emp - ty a - way.
FULL.
He re - membering His mercy, hath holpen His ser - vant Is - ra - el :
Voices in Harmony.
1st and 2d Trebles.
Alto.
as He promised to our forefathers, Abraham and his seed, for - ev - - - er.
Tenor.
Bass.

THE CANTICLES, SET TO GREGORIAN TONES.

Cantate.

THE CANTICLES, SET TO GREGORIAN TONES.

Cantate Domino.—Psalm xcviii.

O - | sing unto the *Lord* a new - song : for *He* hath done marvellous things.
With His own right hand, and *with* His holy arm : hath He *gotten* Himself the victory.
The LORD *declared* His salvation : His righteousness hath He openly *showed* in the sight of the hea — then.
He hath remembered His mercy and truth toward the *house* of Israel : and all the ends of the world have *seen* the salvation of our — God.
Show yourselves joyful unto the Lord, all ye lands : *sing*, rejoice, and give — thanks.
Praise the *Lord* upon the harp : sing to the harp with a *psalm* of thanks — giv — ing.
With *trumpets* also and shawms : O show yourselves *joyful* before the LORD the King.
Let the sea make a noise, and *all* that therein is : the round *world*, and they that dwell therein.
Let the floods clap their hands, and let the hills be joyful *together* before the LORD : *for* He cometh to judge the earth.
With righteousness *shall* He judge the world : and the *people* with - equity.
Glory | be to the *Father*, and to the Son : *and* to the Holy Ghost :
As it | was in the beginning, is *now*, and ever shall be : *world* without end. A — men.

THE CANTICLES, SET TO GREGORIAN TONES.   199

Bonum est confiteri.—Psalm xcii.

It is | a good thing to give *thanks* unto the LORD : and to sing praises unto Thy *Name,* O Most High — est ;

To tell of Thy loving-kindness *early* in the morning : and of Thy *truth* in the night — season ;

Upon an instrument of ten *strings,* and upon the lute : upon a loud *instrument,* and upon the harp.

For Thou, LORD, hast made me *glad* through Thy works : and I will rejoice in giving *praise* for the operations of Thy — hands.

Glory | be to the *Father,* and to the Son : *and* to the Holy Ghost ;

As it | was in the beginning, is *now,* and ever shall be : *world* without end. A — men.

Nunc dimittis.

Nunc dimittis.—St. Luke ii. 29.

Lord — | now lettest Thou Thy *servant* depart in peace — : *ac*cording to Thy word.

For mine eyes have seen — : Thy — salva — tion,

Which *Thou* hast prepared : before the *face* of all — peo — ple ;

To be a *light* to lighten the Gentiles : and to be the glory of *Thy* people Israel.

Glory | be to the *Father*, and to the Son — : *and* to the Holy Ghost ;

As it | was in the beginning, is *now*, and ever shall be : *world* without end. A — men.

(4) Nunc Dimittis.

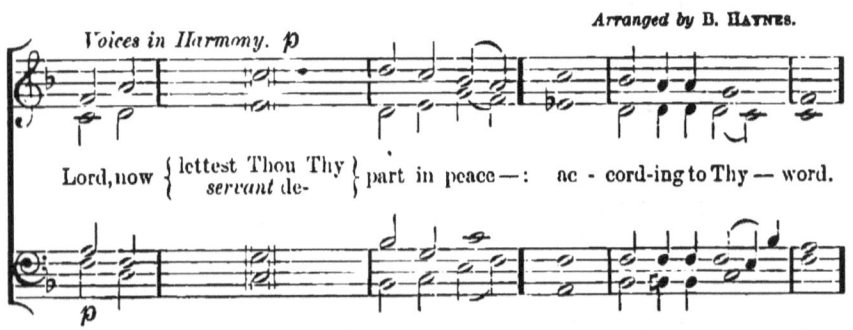

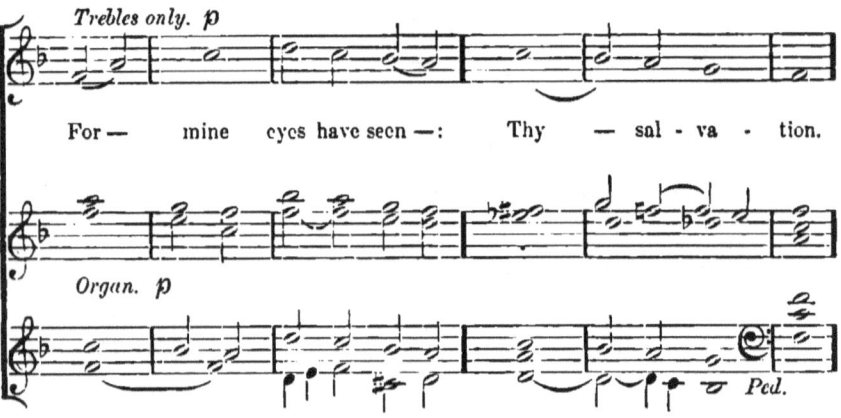

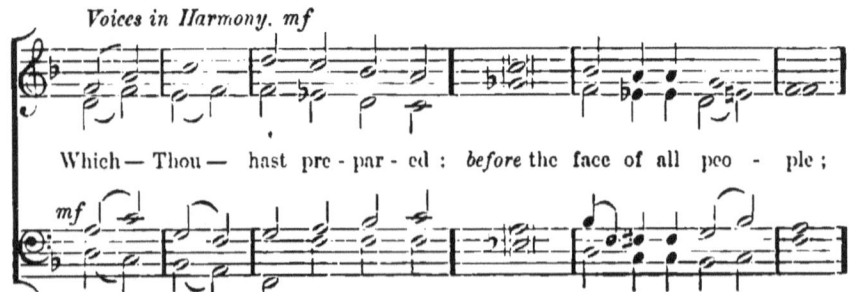

Deus misereatur.

THE CANTICLES, SET TO GREGORIAN TONES. 205

Deus misereatur.—Psalm lxvii.

God be | *merciful* unto us, and bless us : and show us the light of His countenance, *and* be merciful unto us ;

That Thy *way* may be known upon earth — : Thy saving *health* among all na — tions.

Let the people *praise* Thee, O God — : yea, let *all* the people praise — Thee.

O let the nations *rejoice* and be glad — : for Thou shalt judge the folk righteously, and *govern* the nations upon — earth.

Let the people *praise* Thee, O God — : yea, let *all* the people praise — Thee.

Then shall the *earth* bring forth her increase ; and God, even our own God, shall *give* us His bless — ing.

God shall bless — us — : and all the ends of the *world* shall — fear — Him.

Glory | be to the *Father*, and to the Son — : *and* to the Holy Ghost ;

As it | was in the beginning, is *now*, and ever shall be : *world* without end. A — men.

THE CANTICLES, SET TO GREGORIAN TONES.

Benedic.

THE CANTICLES, SET TO GREGORIAN TONES. 207

Benedic, anima mea.—Psalm ciii.

Praise — | the *Lord,* Ò my soul — : and all that is within *me,* praise His holy Name.

Praise the *Lord,* Ò my soul — : and forget *not* all His benefits ;

Who *forgiveth* all thy sin — : and healeth *all* thine infirmities ;

Who saveth thy *life* from destruction : and crowneth thee with *mercy* and loving-kind — ness.

O praise the LORD, ye Angels of His, ye *that* excel in strength — : ye that fulfil His commandment, and hearken *unto* the voice of His — word.

O praise the *Lord,* all ye His hosts — : ye servants of *His* that do His plea — sure.

O speak good of the LORD, all ye works of His, in all *places* of His dominion : praise *thou* the LORD —, O my soul.

Glory | be to the *Father,* and to the Son — : *and* to the Holy Ghost :

As it | was in the beginning, is *now,* and ever shall be : *world* without end. A — men.

PROPER ANTHEMS.

(IN PLACE OF VENITE.)

Easter Day.

PROPER ANTHEMS, SET TO GREGORIAN TONES.

Christ our | Passover is *sacrificed* for — us : *therefore* let us keep the feast ;
Not with the old leaven, neither with the leaven of *malice* and wickedness : but with the unleavened *bread* of sincerity and truth. 1 Cor. v. 7.

Christ being | raised from the *dead*, dieth no more : death hath no *more* dominion over Him.
For in that He died, He *died* unto sin — once : but in that He *liveth*, He liveth unto God.
Likewise reckon ye also yourselves to be dead *indeed* unto sin : but alive unto *God* through Jesus Christ our Lord. *Rom.* vi. 9.

Christ is | *risen* from the dead : and become the *first*-fruits of them that slept.
For *since* by man came death : by man came *also* the resurrection of the dead.
For as in *Adam* all — die : even so in *Christ* shall all be made alive. 1 Cor. xv. 20.

Glory | be to the *Father*, and to the Son : *and* to the Holy Ghost ;
As it | was in the beginning, is *now*, and ever shall be : world without end. A — — — men.

210 PROPER ANTHEMS, SET TO GREGORIAN TONES.

Thanksgiving=Day.

PROPER ANTHEMS, SET TO GREGORIAN TONES. 211

Praise ye | the LORD : for it is good to sing *praises* unto our God : for it is *pleasant,* and praise is come — ly.

The LORD doth build *up* Jerusalem : He gathereth *together* the outcasts of Israel.

He healeth *those* that are broken in heart : *and* bindeth up their wounds.

He covereth the heaven with clouds, and prepareth *rain* for the earth : He maketh the grass to *grow* upon the moun — tains.

He giveth to the *beast* his — food : and to the *young* ravens which — cry.

Praise the LORD, *O* Jerusalem : praise thy *God,* O — Si — on.

For He hath strengthened the *bars* of thy gates : He hath *blessed* thy children within — thee.

He maketh *peace* in thy borders : and filleth thee *with* the finest of the wheat.

Glory | be to the *Father,* and to the Son : *and* to the Holy Ghost ;

As it | was in the beginning, is *now,* and ever shall be : *world* without end. A — men.

Consecration of Churches.

Psalm xxiv.

The earth | is the LORD'S, and all that *therein* is : the compass of the world, and *they* that dwell therein.

For He hath founded *it* upon the seas : and prepared *it* upon the floods.

Who shall ascend into the *hill* of the LORD : or who shall rise up in *His* holy place?

Even he that hath clean hands and a *pure* heart : and that hath not lift up his mind unto vanity, nor *sworn* to deceive his neighbour.

He shall receive the *blessing* from the LORD : and righteousness from the *God* of his salvation.

This is the generation of *them* that seek Him : even of them that *seek* thy face, O Jacob.

Lift up your heads, O ye gates ; and be ye lift up ye *everlasting* doors : and the King of *glory* shall come in.

Who is the *King* of glory : It is the LORD strong and mighty, even the *Lord* mighty in battle.

Lift up your heads, O ye gates ; and be ye lift up, ye *everlasting* doors : and the King of *glory* shall come in.

Who is the *King* of glory : Even the LORD of hosts, *He* is the King of glory.

Glory | be to the Father, *and* to the Son : *and* to the Holy Ghost ;

As it | was in the beginning, is now, and *ever* shall be : world without end. A — men.

Institution of Ministers.

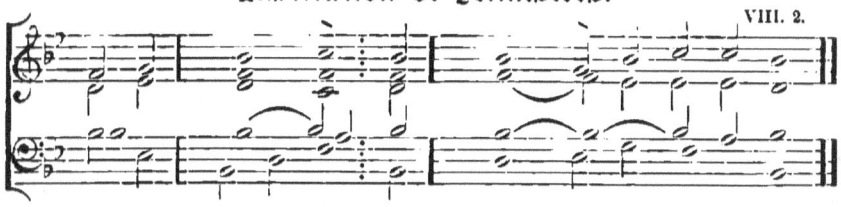

Laudate Nomen.

Praise ye | the Lord, laud ye the *Name* of the Lord : praise it, O *ye* servants of the Lord.

Ye that stand in the *house* of the Lord : in the *courts* of the house of our — God.

O praise the Lord, for the *Lord* is gracious : O sing praises unto His *Name*, for it is love — ly.

The Lord is *gracious* and merciful : long-*suffering*, and of great — good — ness.

The Lord is *loving* unto every man : and His *mercy* is over all His works.

All Thy works praise *Thee*, O Lord : and Thy *saints* give thanks — unto Thee.

The Lord doth build *up* Jerusalem : and gather *together* the outcasts of Israel.

He healeth those that are *broken* in heart : and giveth *medicine* to heal their sick — ness.

The Lord's delight is in *them* that fear Him : and put their *trust* in His mer — cy.

Praise the Lord, *O* Jerusalem : praise thy *God*, O — Zi — on.

For He hath made fast the bars of *thy* gates : and hath *blessed* thy children with in — thee.

He maketh peace in *thy* borders : and filleth *thee* with the flour of wheat.

He is our God, even the God of whom *cometh* salvation : God is the Lord, by whom we escape — death.

O God, wonderful art Thou in Thy *holy* places : even the God of Israel, He will give strength and power unto His *people*. Blessed be — God.

Glory | be to the Father, *and* to the Son : *and* to the Holy Ghost ;

As it | was in the beginning, is now, and *ever* shall be : *world* without end — . A — men.

Miserere.

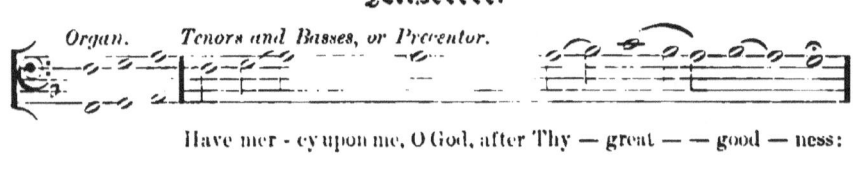
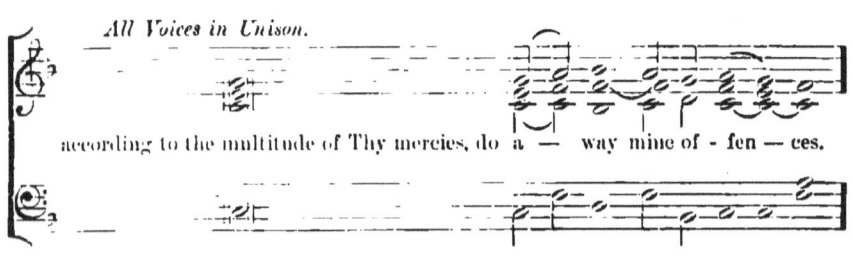

OCCASIONAL ANTHEM, SET TO GREGORIAN TONES.

OCCASIONAL ANTHEM, SET TO GREGORIAN TONES.

then shall they offer young bullocks up — on Thine — al — tar.

Glo - ry — be to the Fa - ther, and to the Son : and —

to the — Ho — ly Ghost; As it was in the beginning, is now, and —

ev - er — shall — be : world with-out end. — A — — — men.

NOTE.—Two modes of chanting this Psalm are here indicated. The first direction at each verse should be continued throughout, or the second throughout.

The harmonies to the barred verses (even numbers) are by Dr. Stainer ; those to the unbarred verses, by the Editor.

De profundis.

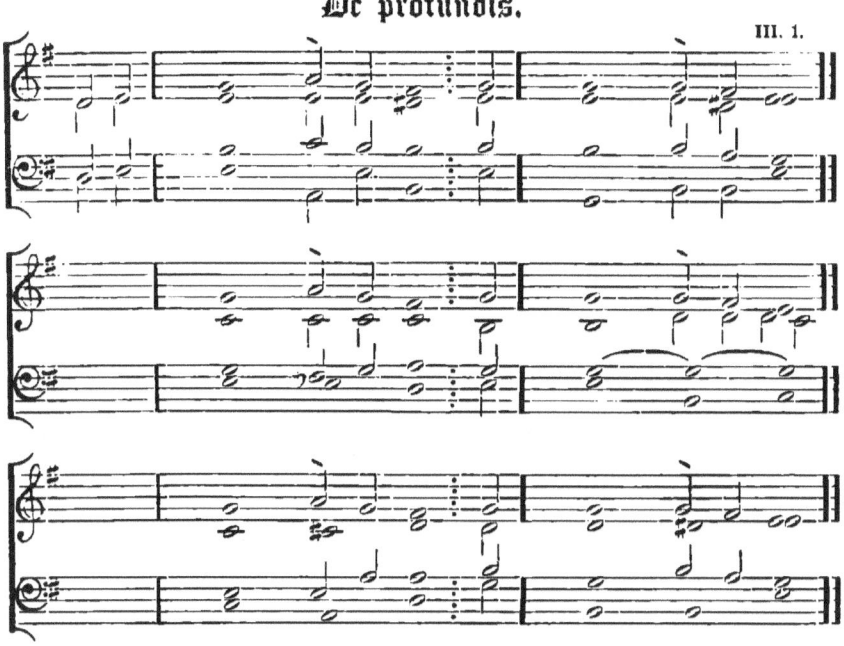

De profundis.—Psalm cxxx.

Out of | the deep have I *called* unto Thee, O LORD : *Lord,* hear my voice.

O let Thine *ears* consider well : the *voice* of my complaint.

If Thou, LORD, wilt be extreme to *mark* what is done amiss : O *Lord,* who may abide it?

For there is *mercy* with — Thee : *therefore* shalt Thou be feared.

I look for the LORD ; my *soul* doth wait for Him : in His *word* is my trust.

My soul *fleeth* unto the Lord : before the morning watch ; I say, *before* the morning watch.

O Israel, trust in the Lord : for with the *Lord* there is mer — cy: and with Him is *plenteous* redemp — tion.

And He shall *redeem* Israel : *from* all his sins.

Glory be to the *Father,* and to the Son : *and* to the Holy Ghost;

As it was in the beginning, is *now*, and ever shall be : world without end. A — men.

INDEX.

	PAGE
AGNUS DEI........*Calkin*..........	90
" ....*Garrett*...........	91
" ....*Bennett*..........	92
" ....*Gounod*..........	94
" ....*Merbecke-Stainer*	123
" ....*Missa de Angelis*	124
AMEN.............*Stainer*..........	103
" ....*Stanford*.......	103
" ....*Selby*...........	104
" ....*Messiter*........	104
APOSTLES' CREED...................	36
BENEDIC.........*Anglican*........	22
" ;..........*Gregorian*.......	206
BENEDICITE.......*Anglican*.......	6
" ....*Gregorian*.......	178
" ....*From Dr. Gauntlett*...........	180
BENEDICTUS DOMINUS.	
" *Anglican*........	8
" *Gregorian*.......	182
" *Stainer (Greg'n)*.	184
" *Parry*...........	135
BENEDICTUS QUI VENIT.	
" *Gounod*.........	86
" *Cobb*............	88
" *Selby*...........	89
" *Plainsong*.......	122
" *Missa de Angelis*.	122
BONUM EST........*Anglican*.....	16
" ....*Gregorian*......	198
BURIAL SERVICE....*Croft*...........	158
" .....*Plainsong*......	163

	PAGE
CANTATE...........*Anglican*........	14
" ....*Gregorian*.......	196
" ....*Bunnett*..........	146
CHORAL SERVICE....*Ferial*..........	31
" ....*Festal*..........	33
COMFORTABLE WORDS, *Plainsong*......	113
CONFESSION........*Harmonized*.....	33
DE PROFUNDIS......*Gregorian*.......	221
DEUS MISEREATUR..*Anglican*........	20
" ..*Gregorian*.......	204
" ..*Bunnett*........	153
GLORIA IN EXCELSIS.*Old Chant*.......	80
" .*Steggall*.........	100
" .*Merbecke*........	126
GLORIA TIBI........(*Various*)........	54
" ....*Plainsong*......	105
I HEARD A VOICE...*Cutler*...... ...	162
" ..*Plainsong*.......	167
JUBILATE..........*Anglican*........	10
" ....*Gregorian*.......	188
" ....*Calkin*..........	140
KYRIE.............*Cobb*............	46
" ....*Messiter*........	47
" ....*Gounod*..........	49
" ....*Gadsby*..........	50
" ....*King Hall*.....	50
" ....*Cobb*............	51
" ....*Schubert*........	51

		PAGE
KYRIE	Benedict	52
"	Field	53
"	Plainsong (1)	105
"	Plainsong (2)	105
LESSER LITANY	Tallys	53
"	Smithe	53
LITANY	Ferial	39
"	Tallys	44
LORD'S PRAYER	Merbecke	96
"	Haynes	98
"	Cantus Solemnis	125
MAGNIFICAT	Anglican	12
"	Gregorian	190
"	Gregory (Greg'n)	192
"	Wesley	143
MISERERE	Gregorian	214
NICENE CREED	Field	55
"	Garrett	59
"	Merbecke	106
"	Gilbert (8th Tone)	110
NUNC DIMITTIS	Anglican	18
"	Gregorian	200
"	Haynes (Greg'n)	202
"	Lloyd	152
OFFERTORY SENTENCES.		
"	Garrett	69
"	Monk	69
"	Gladstone	70
"	Calkin	71
"	Martin	74
"	Martin	76
"	Martin	77
"	Merbecke	112
PROPER PREFACES	Plainsong	116

		PAGE
PROPER ANTHEMS—EASTER.		
"	Anglican	24
"	Gregorian	208
—THANKSGIVING-DAY.		
"	Anglican	25
"	Gregorian	210
—CONSECRATION OF CHURCHES.		
"	Anglican	26
"	Gregorian	212
—INSTITUTION OF MINISTERS.		
"	Anglican	27
"	Gregorian	213
—BURIAL OF THE DEAD.		
"	Anglican	28
"	Gregorian	164
SANCTUS	Aldrich	80
"	Cobb	80
"	Reay	81
"	Croft	83
"	Field	83
"	Tours	84
"	Gounod	85
"	Plainsong	116
SURSUM CORDA	Tallys	78
"	Tours	79
"	Stainer	79
"	Garrett	79
"	Monotone	114
"	Cantus Solemnis	115
TE DEUM	Anglican	4
"	Gregorian	170
"	Iliffe (Greg'n)	172
"	Calkin	129
VENITE	Anglican	2
"	Gregorian	168

www.ingramcontent.com/pod-product-compliance
Lightning Source LLC
Chambersburg PA
CBHW020812230426
43666CB00007B/971